CONTEXTUAL FAMILY THERAPY:
ASSESSMENT AND INTERVENTION PROCEDURES

Peter Goldenthal, PhD, ABPP

King of Prussia, Pennsylvania
and
Wilmington, Delaware

Professional Resource Press
Sarasota, Florida

Published by
Professional Resource Press
(An imprint of the Professional Resource Exchange, Inc.)
Post Office Box 15560
Sarasota, FL 34277-1560

Printed in the United States of America

The copy editor for this book was Patricia Hammond, the managing editor was Debra Fink, the Production Coordinator was Laurie Girsch, and the cover designer was Bill Tabler.

Library of Congress Cataloging-in-Publication Data

Goldenthal, Peter. date.
        Contextual family therapy : assessment and intervention procedures
/ Peter Goldenthal.
                p.   cm. -- (Practitioner's resource series)
        Includes bibliographical references.
        ISBN 0-943158-79-6
        1. Contextual therapy.   2. Contextual therapy--Case studies.
    I. Title.   II. Series.
        [DNLM: 1. Family Therapy--methods.   WM 430.5.F2 G6185c 1993]
    RC488.55.G65   1993
    616.89'156--dc20
    DNLM/DLC
    for Library of Congress   93-10551
                                                                                CIP

For my parents, Carol and Jolene;
My wife, Wendy; and
My children, Rebecca, Sara, and Ariel.

ACKNOWLEDGMENTS

I received a great deal of valuable input in writing this book. Jeff Cebula, Wendy Goldenthal, Sam Knapp, Jamshed Morenas, and Paul Rappaport read earlier versions of the manuscript and provided extremely useful suggestions. Vincent Gioe deserves special recognition; in addition to reviewing the manuscript, he introduced me to contextual therapy and the contextual perspective and suggested that I write the workshop handout that eventually grew into this book.

I owe a particular debt to Dr. Ivan Boszormenyi-Nagy, the founder of the contextual approach, for instruction in contextual therapy, for reading this manuscript and for writing its foreword, and most of all for the many ways in which he has contributed to my professional and personal growth over the years.

Finally I wish to thank Larry Ritt, Debra Fink, and the staff of Professional Resource Press who have been extremely patient, supportive, and helpful throughout this process.

PREFACE TO THE SERIES

As a publisher of books, cassettes, and continuing education programs, the Professional Resource Press and Professional Resource Exchange, Inc. strive to provide mental health professionals with highly applied resources that can be used to enhance clinical skills and expand practical knowledge.

All the titles in the *Practitioner's Resource Series* are designed to provide important new information on topics of vital concern to psychologists, clinical social workers, marriage and family therapists, psychiatrists, and other mental health professionals.

Although the focus and content of each book in this series will be quite different, there will be notable similarities:

1. Each title in the series will address a timely topic of critical clinical importance.

2. The target audience for each title will be practicing mental health professionals. Our authors were chosen for their ability to provide concrete "how-to-do-it" guidance to colleagues who are trying to increase their competence in dealing with complex clinical problems.

3. The information provided in these books will represent "state-of-the-art" information and techniques derived from both clinical experience and empirical research. Each of these guide books will include references and resources for those who wish to pursue more advanced study of the discussed topic.

4. The authors will provide numerous case studies, specific recommendations for practice, and the types of "nitty-gritty" details that clinicians need before they can incorporate new concepts and procedures into their practices.

If there are other topics you would like to see addressed in this series, please let me know.

Lawrence G. Ritt, Publisher

FOREWORD

Contextual therapy, an empirically developed basic understanding of relating and of therapy, is often misunderstood as theoretical. This is especially unfortunate because every theoretical
facet of contextual therapy originates from and is validated
through systematic observation of individual, family, or couples
therapy. Therefore the rich illustrative/clinical materials of this
book provide a very useful contribution to the literature. It is a
helpful reading even for the reader who is familiar with the basic
texts of the approach.

Dr. Goldenthal is a clinical psychologist and a well-versed
therapist of families, therefore of both adults and children. In
addition, he has been a teacher in the Department of Human Development at Bryn Mawr College and in the Department of Psychology at the University of Pennsylvania.

For a number of years Dr. Goldenthal has studied and also
taught the contextual therapy approach. He was an analytically
minded student of the approach and became an effective practitioner in its application.

Dr. Goldenthal is among the growing number of contempo-
rary American and European therapists who have a capacity and
motivation to think through the implications of contextual therapy
and seriously apply it in specific fields. He is one who has been
able to grasp and distinguish the ethical dimension of relationship

as a key therapeutic factor. The illustrations from his practice will help the reader to see how many contextual principles may be applied in working with families in general and with children in particular.

Ivan Boszormenyi-Nagy, MD

ABSTRACT

Contextual therapy is an integrative, intergenerational, multilateral, and resource-oriented approach to helping individuals, couples, and families. This book focuses on the needs of practicing clinicians and emphasizes the practical and clinical application of contextual concepts and procedures. The contextual approach, developed over the past 30 years by Ivan Boszormenyi-Nagy, MD, focuses on resources rather than on pathology, on acknowledgment rather than blame, and on future possibilities rather than on past errors. The contextual framework comprises four dimensions: individual and family history, individual psychological issues, family transactions and power issues, and issues related to fairness in relationships. The approach emphasizes the importance of understanding how harm which has befallen individuals in the past can lead to a reliance on destructive entitlement and to a tendency to parentify others, especially children.

The approach also emphasizes the importance of helping people to identify and use resources for giving and receiving in their families. Clinical vignettes illustrate major concepts and procedures used in contextual assessment and intervention including: the right to give, loyalty and split loyalty, injustice, destructive entitlement, parentification, acknowledgment, lending weight, and exoneration. The sequence of steps involved in contextual assessment is described, as is the transition between assessment and intervention phases. Multidirected partiality is the most basic contextual principle and underlies all assessment and intervention activities. This principle is illustrated as it is used in conducting assessment and intervention with families. Intervention procedures are illustrated as they are applied in a number of different clinical situations, including the treatment of families who seek treatment as the result of their children having engaged in disruptive behaviors. The resource orientation of the contextual approach is emphasized throughout as is the emphasis on acknowledging the efforts made by all generations toward relating to each other in considerate ways despite having experienced injustice in their own lives.

TABLE OF CONTENTS

BASIC CONCEPTS OF
FAIRNESS IN RELATIONSHIPS *(Continued)*

INTERVENTION PROCEDURES *(Continued)*

CONTEXTUAL FAMILY THERAPY: ASSESSMENT AND INTERVENTION PROCEDURES

BACKGROUND

Contextual therapy, a method of treatment applicable to individuals, couples, and families, is the product of three decades of work by Ivan Boszormenyi-Nagy* and his colleagues. This book is geared to the interests of the practicing clinician and so provides only a brief overview of the conceptual basis of this approach before going into clinical practice issues. A number of excellent sources discuss the theoretical foundations of the model in greater detail (e.g., Boszormenyi-Nagy, 1965, 1987; Boszormenyi-Nagy, Grunebaum, & Ulrich, 1991; Boszormenyi-Nagy & Krasner, 1986; Boszormenyi-Nagy & Spark, 1973).

Boszormenyi-Nagy trained as a physician and psychiatrist in his native country of Hungary and immigrated to the United States in 1950. In 1957 he started a clinical research inpatient unit devoted to the treatment of psychotic patients at the Eastern Pennsylvania Psychiatric Institute (EPPI). This unit later became the Department of Family Psychiatry and provided family therapy training to many who later became leaders in the field. Initially

---

*Boszormenyi-Nagy is pronounced as if it were spelled Bessormainee-Nahj and is sometimes shortened in the literature to Nagy.

1

utilizing intensive individual psychotherapeutic approaches, Boszormenyi-Nagy soon began to hold regular therapy sessions with his psychotic patients and their families.

Boszormenyi-Nagy credits the influences of Kalman Gyarfas, Freud's writings, Ronald Fairbairn, and the existential philosophers. In addition, Boszormenyi-Nagy had ongoing exchanges with others who were also at the forefront of the family therapy movement, including Murray Bowen, Lyman Wynne, Nathan Ackerman, Carl Whitaker, and Don Jackson (Boszormenyi-Nagy & Krasner, 1986).

Contextual therapy is intergenerational, integrative, multilateral, and oriented toward resources and the future. It is intergenerational in its concern for understanding the individual and family contexts of members of at least three generations, an aspect of contextual therapy that will be discussed in detail in subsequent sections. It is multilateral in seeking to understand and to be partial to all the people whose lives are likely to be affected by what happens in the therapy. It is integrative in drawing on dynamic formulations, particularly those associated with the object relations theorists (e.g., Fairbairn, 1954; Guntrip, 1961) and those associated with family systems approaches. In addition, Buber's (1958) concept of the "dialogue" occupies a prominent place in the elaboration of the contextual concept of mutually collaborative meeting in relationships. Contextual therapy is above all resource oriented; it focuses the therapist's attention, and seeks to focus family members' attention, on strengths rather than pathology, on crediting rather than blaming, and on exploring possibilities for enhancing relationships by focusing on the potential for considerate giving and receiving.

Although contextual therapy draws on both individual psychodynamic and family systems sources, it cannot adequately be understood by reference to either alone. It differs from psychoanalytic approaches in its focus on current, as well as past, interpersonal relationships and on the need for action in changing those relationships in the present. It differs from many family therapy approaches in its attention to individual dynamics and to individuals' needs for fairness.

This integration of psychodynamic object relations thinking with family systems formulations has led to criticism of Boszormenyi-Nagy's work by some who view themselves as more "purely" systemic in their thinking. Hoffman (1981), for example, criticizes the contextual approach for incorporating psychodynamic thinking and for being "historical" and "linear," in contrast to "those who made a sharper break with the therapeutic establishment: the ecological, structural, strategic, and systemic schools" (p. 255). Without going too deeply into the debate about the meaning and significance of distinctions between linearity and circularity, it is interesting to note Wynne's (1988) comment regarding the concept of circularity: "On the terminologic level the metaphor of circularity ignores the lineality [sic] of time and therefore is inaccurate" (p. 271).

Levant's (1984) classification scheme provides a useful framework with which to contrast the contextual model with other prominent and well-known approaches to therapy with families. In this brief section I shall not attempt to be exhaustive but rather to highlight some of the major differences. From Levant's perspective it makes sense to group the contextual approach with others that place emphasis on understanding the family over an intergenerational time frame. These "historical" approaches include the psychodynamic family therapies of Ackerman (1966), Framo (1976, 1982), and Wynne (1965) as well as the multigenerational approach of Bowen and his colleagues (Bowen, 1966). In addition to the emphasis on the importance of family history, these approaches have in common a desire to lead or "coach" families rather than to direct them to change. They also pay attention, to a greater or lesser degree, to individual psychodynamics.

In my experience, this integration of individual and family systems thinking, and of historical understanding with an emphasis on present and future action, makes the contextual approach especially useful. I have found the ability to draw on both formulations regarding individual psychodynamics and patterns of power, transactions, and communication in families - all within one integrated framework - to be very helpful. When these two complementary frameworks are combined with Boszormenyi-Nagy's formulations regarding fairness in relationships, the result is a comprehensive and powerful therapeutic model. As will be illustrated in later case examples, the approach allows the therapist to address the reality, intrapersonal, interpersonal, and ethical aspects of problems that lead people to seek help.

The contextual approach can be applied to work with individuals, couples, or families, as its essence lies in helping people to act based on fair consideration of other people's needs, a goal which need not require the presence of every family member in the therapy room. In conducting seminars and workshops, however, I have found that the contextual approach can be made clearest by discussing concepts and illustrating procedures using families with children as exemplars. I have adopted the same approach here and chosen to illustrate procedures using families with children, often families with young children. In the sections on assessment and intervention I mention some alterations in practice which the therapist can make to accommodate treatment in which only one or two people actively participate.

FOUR-DIMENSIONAL FRAMEWORK

From a contextual perspective, people can best be understood and helped if the therapist appreciates four aspects of each person's life and relationships, typically referred to as *dimensions*:

Dimension 1. Existential Facts (referred to later as the dimension of individual and family history)
Dimension 2. Psychology
Dimension 3. Family Transactions and Power
Dimension 4. Relational Fairness

The concept of dimensions differs from the more familiar notion of "levels" in that the four dimensions are simultaneous and there is no assumption that any one dimension is "deeper" than any other. Neither is it assumed that assessment or intervention on any one level is more important than that on any other dimension. Fairness issues dominate discussions of contextual practice, but not because these issues have greater importance than, for example, facts regarding a family's ethnicity or an understanding of one person's cognitive impairment, struggle with schizophrenia, or history of severe abuse during childhood. Rather, contextual therapists look to issues of fairness in family relationships for guidance when faced with difficult decisions regarding possible interventions. For this reason "aspect" is a more accurate synonym for dimension than "level." The integrative (individual as well as systems) nature of the contextual approach leads therapists to think about all family members (not just an "identified patient") in terms of these four dimensions.

THE EXISTENTIAL DIMENSION

This dimension refers to the "facts" of a person's life. These include biological facts (e.g., being born male or female, being a twin, or having a chronic illness or a physical handicap); historical facts (e.g., being an only child, a daughter in a family of six sons, or a child whose mother died in childbirth); racial and cultural facts (e.g., being Irish, Native American, African American, or Jewish); as well as more personal facts (e.g., having lost a parent at an early age, having grown up with divorced parents, having an alcoholic parent). In conducting therapy according to contextual guidelines, awareness and appreciation of the existential aspect of clients' lives is essential to the process of uncovering *injustice,* a procedure which will be discussed later.

THE PSYCHOLOGICAL DIMENSION

Unlike some family therapy approaches that do not focus on the individuals who make up family systems, the contextual approach places importance on assessing the cognitive and emotional functioning of these individuals. In assessing people on the psychological dimension, a contextually oriented therapist remembers that, although families may be systems, systems are also made up of individuals who have thoughts, feelings, and complex inner lives. In other words, individuals are systems too.

The contextual model, while relying on considerations of relational fairness for the greatest source of therapeutic leverage, recognizes the importance of respecting individual differences in capacity and current functioning. These differences include those characteristic of traditional psychodynamically oriented therapies such as ego strengths and weaknesses, character structure, ego defenses, and coping style. They also include diagnostic formulations regarding the presence or absence of significant levels of anxiety or depression, thought disorder, or personality disorder. This is also the dimension that integrates developmental considerations including those discussed by Anna Freud (1946), Erikson (1963, 1968, 1980), and Piaget (1963; Flavell, 1977; Piaget & Inhelder, 1969).

Many contextual therapists use nonpsychodynamic concepts as well. I often find it useful to draw on Rotter's (1954) social learning theory concepts (e.g., expectancies, minimal goal level). Others who wish to use the contextual approach in their work may find it helpful to incorporate concepts they have become familiar with in their work as cognitive, behavioral, or client-centered therapists.

THE DIMENSION OF TRANSACTIONS AND POWER

This dimension draws on family systems concepts and observations. These include patterns of communication among family members, triangulation, coalitions, boundaries within the family and between the family and the environment, family roles and the potential for scapegoating, and issues of interpersonal power and control. In this sense this dimension draws on the observations of many family therapists and writers on family therapy such as Jackson (1957), Bowen (1978), Wynne (1965), and Bateson and his colleagues (Bateson et al., 1956) as well as more recent contributors such as Minuchin (1974), Haley (1976), and Selvini-Palazzoli and her colleagues (Selvini-Palazzoli et al., 1978). Discussion of these family systems issues is available in a number of sources (e.g., Gurman & Kniskern, 1981, 1991; Levant, 1984).

THE DIMENSION OF FAIRNESS IN BALANCING
GIVE AND TAKE IN RELATIONSHIPS

This dimension is central to the contextual approach. In some writings on the subject it is referred to as the "ethical dimension," perhaps leading to the impression that a therapist is supposed to know right from wrong and to instruct families in how to behave properly. Actually, the therapist's role is to help individuals and families to think about the fairness of their actions rather than to tell them what is fair and what is not fair. In other words, the idea of thinking about relational ethics does not imply that anyone, least of all the therapist, prescribes a code of behavior for others to follow. It involves instead striving for balance between giving and receiving for all those people involved in a relationship.

The use of the word "ethics" may also lead some people to believe that this approach is somehow very "philosophical," and that the therapy involves people in a great deal of theorizing about such issues as "fairness" and "loyalty." In my own work, this is quite far from the truth. In fact, I think of issues of fairness as being more closely linked to action than to theorizing. One helps people to think about fairness so that they can do something to increase the fairness of their relationships. Although insight into oneself and one's relationships can be very helpful, direct action that brings relationships closer to a balance of fairness is always necessary. Within this framework issues of fairness and relational ethics are far from theoretical.

The only way to determine where fairness lies in a particular situation is for all involved persons to consider the impact of their actions on others and to try to discover what the other person's concerns are. One's guesses or intuitions about what another's concerns might be or should be do not provide sufficient guidance to make this sort of determination. Individuals in relationships must actually work hard to find out what the other person sees as being central to his or her interest. The therapist's job is to encourage clients to examine the balance of give and take in their relationships with others, not to serve as a voice of authority regarding right and wrong. As will be seen in later sections, when therapists guide clients to think about fairness in their marital or family relationships, questions about loyalty and especially conflicting loyalties to parents, spouses, and children often arise.

DISTINCTIONS BETWEEN
FAIRNESS AND OTHER DIMENSIONS

It may sometimes be unclear whether a given concept refers to the psychological, transactional, or ethical aspect of reality. In distinguishing between the psychological and ethical aspects of a person's life, it may help to think about the difference between concepts referring to unique personality characteristics and those reflecting the quality of a relationship with regard to the fairness of exchange in that relationship. For example, the psychological concept of trust may refer to a person's tendency to believe what others say, in other words, to a *feeling* of trust in another (e.g., Rotter, 1954). The ethical concept of *trustworthiness*, on the other hand, refers to reliable, responsible, and considerate action and is in this sense a relational, rather than a psychological, concept. To further complicate things, "trust" may also refer more to power and control than to actual trustworthiness, as in the case of a Mafia chieftain who asks his underling, "Can we trust (i.e., control) this guy?"

In the section on assessment I will be talking in detail about the assessment of *constructive* and *destructive entitlement* as concepts of fairness in relationships. Understanding a person's feelings of entitlement (an aspect of psychological assessment) may be of equal importance in some cases. To anticipate a bit, a person may feel very entitled - sometimes referred to colloquially as an "overentitled person" - and yet be heavily relying on destructive entitlement. Another person may experience low self-esteem, feelings of low self-worth, and depression as one manifestation of feeling "unentitled" while actually having earned a great deal of constructive entitlement.

BASIC CONCEPTS OF
FAIRNESS IN RELATIONSHIPS

THE RIGHT TO GIVE

Contextual therapy is grounded in some basic beliefs about family life. Newborns are literally helpless; very young children are essentially helpless. Both depend totally on their parents. The relative helplessness of children diminishes over time but persists as dependency until adulthood. During this prolonged period of dependency children receive more from their parents (beginning with the gift of life itself) than they will ever be able to repay. Despite the undeniable fact that parents give more to children than they can repay, beginning to give to parents in return, and having the opportunity to give, is a crucial part of normal development.

In other words, this approach assumes that children have a *right to give* to their parents. Ideally this giving is developmentally appropriate and on the child's terms. The forms of such giving change as a child develops. For an infant this may mean smiling in response to a mother's smile or cooing in response to a father's talking. A toddler may offer a favorite toy to his or her parents, or spontaneously offer to share a cookie. School-age children typically give to their parents partially through their accomplishments, a form of giving that may persist through adulthood.

The emphasis on the right to give reflects observations of children who consistently manifest a desire to give something of relational value to their parents, even if those parents have failed to even minimally meet the child's needs for nurturance, safety, and support. From a contextual perspective, the right to give is at least as important as the right to receive, because giving leads to earned merit and to greater self-validation in a developing youngster. The vignette of "Joey" illustrates how powerful a child's wish to give to a parent can be and how much it may violate commonly accepted notions of what is "good" for children.

Joey: A Child's Right to
Give to an "Abusive" Mother (Vignette #1)*

One afternoon, 6-year-old Joey, seeing his psychotic mother about to cut her wrists with a knife, took the knife away from her and hid it. His mother then took a second knife from a drawer. When Joey attempted to take away the second knife, his mother threw him down on the bed and, apparently in response to an auditory hallucination, stabbed him repeatedly. Fortunately none of the stab wounds was fatal and Joey recovered after several weeks in the hospital.

In individual therapy sessions Joey frequently spoke of his mother. Once he told the therapist, "I love my mommy, but I don't think I should live with her now." During a session in early February, he asked the therapist's help in making a valentine for his mother, and began to talk of his wish to have visits with his mother, who was at that time in a locked ward in a psychiatric hospital. The therapist saw this wish to make a valentine and to visit the mother as a concrete and developmentally appropriate way of giving and as a demonstration of the powerful motive for children to give to parents.

---

*Names and all identifying characteristics of persons in all case examples have been disguised thoroughly to protect privacy.

As children mature they are naturally able to give more to their parents. It is important that parents provide opportunities for children to do this. It is also important that each parent foster the child's freedom to give to the other parent. In intact and well-functioning families this may be easy. In the case of separation, divorce, remarriage, and especially adoption, parents (including stepparents and foster parents) will need to work to allow their children to give freely to the estranged, invisible, or missing parent or parents. The emphasis on the benefits that accrue to adults through being partial to the rights and needs of absent parent figures represents an important difference between the contextual approach to working with separated and divorced families and many other therapies.

The concept of a child's right to give to his or her parents has many important implications for carrying out contextual therapy. One implication is that a child's development will be harmed if that child is unable to give to both parents due to a severe *loyalty conflict,* a phenomenon discussed in detail in the section on loyalty. In addition, although developmentally appropriate giving is crucial to children's well-being, coerced, premature, or disproportionate giving by children to parents can be harmful. Parents sometimes rely on young children for emotional support or to meet their needs for affection, security, or intimacy which either are not met in other areas of their lives or were not met when they were children. Overreliance on one's children is basically a form of exploitation or *parentification* and is discussed in detail in the sections on contextual assessment and intervention.

AN INTERGENERATIONAL PERSPECTIVE

The people whom I have referred to as "parents" up to this point were once children themselves, just as many of those I have referred to as "children" will become parents in the future. Contextual therapy's emphasis on exploring family history reflects the importance of each individual's connections to his or her parents, grandparents, and great-grandparents, as well as to his or her children, grandchildren, and great-grandchildren. Parents who themselves received adequate parenting will be able to nurture, guide, and support their children's development and so will acquire *merit* and earn *constructive entitlement* that will ultimately benefit their descendants as well as themselves.

The contextual approach emphasizes intergenerational connections in both directions - the past and the future. Many of the procedures which will be discussed later may appear to focus on previous generations. The underlying goal, however, is to benefit present, and above all, future, generations. This concern for the future, implicit in many therapies, is made explicit in contextual work. Action, especially action outside the therapy room, is an essential ingredient of the contextual approach.

LOYALTY

From a contextual perspective, it is important to distinguish between *feeling* loyal to someone and *being* loyal to that person. Loyalty refers to an obligation to another person with whom one is in close relationship, and so is an ethical concept. Feelings of loyalty, while important, rightfully belong to the domain of psychology; coerced loyalty - basically a form of obedience - belongs to the realm of transactions and power.

Loyalty is inherently relative. People express their loyalty for each other through their preferential treatment of each other relative to others to whom they relate less preferentially. One's loyalty to one's spouse, parents, or children will naturally be greater than one's loyalty to a co-worker or other acquaintance. As will be discussed in the following sections, difficulties arise when these loyalties to family members conflict with each other. It is important to note that a child's or adult's loyalty to his or her parents reflects his or her need to be loyal; it is not dependent on the parent having earned the loyalty through exemplary, or even adequate, parenting. Some of the most dramatic examples of children's loyalty to their parents occur in the absence of any obvious signs of giving from the parent to the child.

Loyalty may be visible in such obvious areas as an adult's adherence to his or her parents' religion, political party, values, trade, or profession, or in a child's open display of affection or admiration for his or her parents. Loyalties can also be *invisible*. These loyalties are indirect rather than direct. A man whose father was an alcoholic may never touch alcohol but at the same time may be a workaholic who spends 70 to 80 hours a week at his job. A woman who received harsh and unjust criticism and rejection as a child may express much anger toward her parents and be committed to being different from them in every way possible. And yet, she may find herself being impatient with her children's age-appropriate playfulness and harsh in her criticism of even their smallest mistakes. In this way she may be invisibly loyal to her parents by behaving in the same harsh manner with her children as her parents did with her.

Adults often experience considerable distress when they must choose one parent over another, whatever the reason. Children have even more powerful developmental needs to be able to experience nonconflicting loyalties to both parents. When a child's loyalty to one parent causes the child to be disloyal to the other parent, the severe conflict is referred to as *split loyalty*. Disloyalty to one parent or the other creates serious relational imbalances and emotional and psychological distress. Split loyalty can result when a child's father and mother cannot maintain a trustworthy relationship or when one parent cannot tolerate the child's loyalty to the other parent. The presence of severe split loyalty in late childhood or adolescence, particularly when combined with depression and lack of hope about the situation improving, constitutes a significant risk factor for suicidal behavior.

Split loyalty can also occur when there is a mistrustful relationship between a parent and a stepparent or between a temporary foster parent and a biological parent. Children may also experience split loyalty in intact families characterized by mistrustful relationships. Although divorce and split loyalty are not synonymous, highly conflictual divorces in which child custody and visitation are disputed can easily lead children to experience split loyalty. On the other hand, if divorce leads to an increase of trustworthiness it may also reduce the intensity of the children's loyalty conflicts. Unfortunately, the impact of mistrust between adults who are responsible for the care of young children can have an impact on the children that persists into adulthood and may be seen in their own marital and parenting difficulties. For this reason it is also important to consider the possible impact of split loyalty on adult clients who may present themselves as having "individual issues."

When parents do not trust each other, children sometimes must choose the parent to whom they will be more loyal. The following brief descriptions of therapy sessions illustrate this.

Sheila and Robbie:
<u>Two Case Illustrations of Split Loyalty</u>

Sheila, age 12, was referred due to a marked drop in her grades following her parents' separation. Sheila's mother had begun a new relationship and wanted to take Sheila and her 7-year-old brother with her and her new companion on a trip. Sheila's father objected very strongly to this and insisted on the matter being settled in court where he hoped that a judge would ask Sheila her preference regarding going on the trip or not. In a session prior to the planned hearing, Sheila said, "No way do I want to go to court. I'd be up there and mom would be looking at me and saying 'say yes,' and dad would be looking at me and saying 'say no.' "

Robbie, age 10, had also been referred for school problems following parental separation, although his problems involved disruptive behavior combined with a pattern of not completing his homework. Sessions also included Robbie's mother and his 7-year-old sister. After many sessions, during which Robbie typically feigned boredom or disinterest in the family discussion, Robbie said, "Y'know how when you ask me about stuff with my dad I always say 'sort of ' or 'kinda,' well that's what I usually do with him so he won't get mad."

The section on *constructive* and *destructive entitlement* will discuss the ways in which what superficially may appear to be "bad parenting" may actually reflect parents' inabilities to see their children's developmental needs as the direct result of their own life experiences. It is futile to cajole or exhort adults who are divorcing to be more considerate of their children before trying to see things as these adults do. From the perspective of a man who never knew his father and who was abandoned by his mother as a toddler, asking a child to testify in court that he prefers one parent over the other may seem totally appropriate. The principle of *multidirected partiality* leads the contextual therapist to look for the injustice in these adults' lives - including being subjected to parentification (see next section) when they were children - which has led them to rely on destructive entitlement instead of a more constructive entitlement. Split loyalty always involves a destructive form of *parentification.*

DESTRUCTIVE PARENTIFICATION

A distinction can be made between Minuchin's (1974) concept of the *parental child* and the concept of *destructive parentification,* or more simply, *parentification,* referred to in this model. A parental child (Minuchin, 1974) is one who joins the parental subsystem, being granted a certain degree of quasiparental power in the process. As Minuchin points out, this can have positive effects, helping a child to develop greater maturity and a heightened sense of responsibility. As he also points out, however, too much quasiparental responsibility can be harmful, particularly if it interferes with normal development and socialization. The idea of a parental child, which focuses on power, is a transactional concept. *Destructive parentification,* on the other hand, is an ethical concept and focuses on the balance of fairness in relationships. Merely having some parent-like roles does not necessarily constitute parentification. As we shall see in a later section, a parentified person, whether child or adult, is called upon to act like the selflessly giving parent of another person. In the case of a parentified child, this most often means that the child becomes the parent to his or her own parent.

THERAPEUTIC LEVERAGE

Although psychological, factual, and systemic considerations are important, the dominant source of therapeutic leverage in the contextual approach arises from thinking about the balance of give and take, that is, from reliance on the ethical dimension. The key concepts here are those of *loyalty, constructive entitlement* (sometimes referred to in contextual writings simply as *entitlement*), *destructive entitlement,* and *disentitlement.* Reliance on *constructive entitlement* is seen in a person's concern for the ways in which his or her actions affect others (particularly the ways in which they affect or have the potential to affect his or her children) and from acting in accordance with this concern. Individuals acquire merit (an ethical term) through responsible giving, and as the result of this acquired merit also gain self-validation and the psychological benefits of increased personal security and freedom.

CONSTRUCTIVE ENTITLEMENT

Just as the recipient of responsible giving benefits from what he or she is given, so does the giver benefit through an actual increase in self-worth, through gaining merit. Psychologically the giver, who earns constructive entitlement, benefits through enhanced security and freedom while the person who receives incurs an obligation for future repayment of some kind.

DESTRUCTIVE ENTITLEMENT

The idea that someone might be entitled to be destructive sounds contradictory on its surface. After all, who could possibly be entitled to be destructive? Perhaps the clearest way to understand this apparent paradox is to consider a child who has been diagnosed with a debilitating and potentially life-threatening illness like diabetes or sickle cell anemia. There is no sense in which such a youngster can be said to have brought the illness on himself or herself, no sense in which the youngster deserves the illness, and no sense in which it is fair. On the other hand, the youngster is clearly entitled to a better life, is entitled to a normal lifespan, is entitled to be angry with his or her parents and all adults for the unfairness of his or her condition, and is even entitled to want someone to take the blame for the illness. Of course, at the same time nobody is really entitled to act destructively toward others as the result of the injustice that has occurred in their lives.

The clinical indications of relying on destructive *entitlement* include a lack of sensitivity, caring, or concern for others' needs, feelings, hopes, and misfortunes. The person who relies on destructive entitlement is also particularly insensitive to the ways in which his or her actions affect others. All individuals occasionally do things that hurt others; this does not necessarily represent destructive entitlement, only human frailty. People who rely predominantly on destructive entitlement in relating to others, however, have experienced so much injustice themselves that they have become blind to the harm that they cause to others. A father who described the injustices he had suffered as a child was asked if he hoped that things would be better for his children than they had been for him. The extent of his reliance on destructive entitlement was manifested in his response, "Why should they be?"

RELIANCE ON CONSTRUCTIVE VERSUS DESTRUCTIVE ENTITLEMENT

I would like to anticipate a possible confusion regarding constructive and destructive entitlement. It may appear that the two factors are independent, reflecting two more or less unique life circumstances; some people have constructive entitlement, others have only destructive entitlement. In fact everybody accumulates destructive entitlement. So the crucial question is not so much whether or not a person "has" destructive entitlement or "how much" of it he or she has. The question is rather the extent to which people rely on destructive entitlement in their relationships with others as opposed to the extent to which they are able to rely on constructive entitlement.

A man who cannot see the value in his children's having a better life than he did must have experienced severe injustice in his own life. It must have been severe enough, in fact, to prevent him from seeing what would benefit his children. His destructive entitlement was not merely the result of emotional or physical deprivation. Poverty or parental absence due to the need to work long hours do not necessarily lead to destructive entitlement. It is the experience of unfairness and injustice, rather, that produces destructive entitlement. Physical violence directed against children, especially when accompanied by the belief that the child "had it coming," is one manifestation of this sort of blindness.

It is well known that parents who abuse their children were likely to have been abused in childhood themselves. From the perspective offered here, the injustice of their own victimization has made it impossible for them to see that they are victimizing others. This is the blindness of destructive entitlement. Constructive entitlement, in contrast, leads to responsible giving, which is based on considering the consequences for others, especially for children who are in the family or are yet to be born.

16

Destructive entitlement is not merely the result of inadequate parenting. It results, rather, from the experience of injustice in one's life, usually one's early life. It may result from events for which no ready blame can be found, such as the very early loss of a parent or being born with a disability or other severe handicap. Destructive entitlement can result from a variety of factors: parental alcoholism; sexual, physical, or emotional abuse; or psychological or actual abandonment. Destructive entitlement can also result from being victimized by oppression, institutionalized injustice, or war.

People act based on their entitlement. Constructive entitlement leads a person to enter into responsible give-and-take relationships. Destructive entitlement leads a person to act unilaterally in ways that may be destructive to others. By contrast, a disentitled person differs in being unable to act in either a constructive or a destructive manner; the person is essentially frozen in inaction. This disentitled person is frozen because he or she cannot give.

Although all individuals, especially infants and children, need to receive from others, all individuals also have a need to give. Each person has a right and a need to give to others, and, as discussed in an earlier section, a child's need to give to parents in developmentally appropriate ways is as important as the right to receive, because it is through giving that the child will be able to earn entitlement and to validate himself or herself. True giving grows out of consideration for another's needs, including the other person's need to give in return, and so leads to increased merit. Giving which does not consider the recipient, however, can actually be more harmful than helpful. Disproportionate giving, while it may appear to be altruistic and generous, binds rather than frees both the giver and the receiver and may be thought of as a form of *destructive overgiving.*

A middle-aged man talked about his sadness as a child in witnessing his father's distress over not having the financial resources to provide for his children as he wished to. Now a successful businessman, this man took great pride in giving generously to his own children. In fact, his desire to protect his teenage son from feeling responsible for him, as he had for his father, made it difficult for the son to find room to give to the father. Father often told his teenage son that neither father nor mother needed anything from him, that they were self-sufficient and ready to give anything their son needed, materially or otherwise. Although it is very hard to fault parents who wish to give to their children, parental giving without providing opportunities to give in return may diminish a young person's ability to acquire merit.

Put more psychologically, being denied the opportunity to give can stifle a young person's self-esteem, sense of autonomy, and self-mastery. This example illustrates one way in which the injustice that a father experienced in his childhood can make it difficult for him to see that his efforts to be a good parent may inadvertently interfere with his child's growth.

GENERAL PRINCIPLES OF CONTEXTUAL ASSESSMENT AND INTERVENTION

HOW ASSESSMENT ISSUES BLEND INTO TREATMENT ISSUES

In this as in nearly all forms of treatment, the boundary between assessment and intervention is often blurred. With the possible exception of psychological testing or highly structured behavioral assessment techniques, nearly any evaluative technique will also have some effect as an intervention. Asking a client to "begin at the beginning" in relating a concern may have the effect of reassuring the person that the therapist is interested, has time for the client, and believes that he or she can help. The connection between assessment and intervention is particularly true of the model I am presenting here. A question asked in the first 5 minutes of the first session may have as much power as an intervention as anything said for the next 5 or 10 sessions.

The assessment of fairness issues such as injustice, constructive and destructive entitlement, loyalty, and particularly acknowledgment, often blend into intervention. Questions about family history and about possible connections between family history and current difficulties are useful from an assessment standpoint. To the extent that they begin to enhance awareness of loyalty issues and people's own histories of being unfairly exploited, these are also intervention techniques. In the sections describing assessment procedures I will indicate those which are also particularly important intervention procedures. The intervention procedures themselves will be presented in detail later.

MULTIDIRECTED PARTIALITY

Both contextual assessment and intervention rely heavily on the use of *multidirected partiality*, the most basic contextual procedure. This requires the therapist to work hard to see a situation from the perspectives of each of the individuals who are likely to be affected by the course of therapy. In addition to those actually participating in the therapy, this typically includes parents, separated spouses, and potentially children and grandchildren. This procedure differs from therapeutic neutrality (the avoidance of siding with anyone) or unidirected partiality (the siding with one family member against all others).

In addition to being interested in the facts of each client's life circumstances, history, and individual psychological makeup, the contextual therapist has a particular interest in issues relevant to relational fairness. In attempting to be partial to each family member, the therapist may encounter situations in which it is difficult to side with a person's present behavior, for example, in the case of a parent who is being abusive or neglectful to young children. In such cases it is useful to explore the past injustices that led to the parent's inability to see the harm he or she is causing his or her children. This process allows the therapist to be partial to the person without being partial to his or her present actions.

Before discussing those aspects of assessment which are unique to the contextual approach, I will describe some structuring techniques I have found to be both practical and useful. I then discuss some practical issues involved in both the assessment and treatment phases of conducting contextual therapy followed by discussion of procedures for conducting the assessment.

STRUCTURING TECHNIQUES

Contextual therapy, like all other forms of psychotherapy, relies on the establishment of a trusting and, above all, a *trustworthy* relationship between the therapist and clients. From a contextual perspective, promising results, or simply encouraging clients to "trust" at the beginning of therapy runs counter to the goal of being trustworthy. The goal of initial sessions is rather to gather enough information about the client and the client's context to make an informed judgment about the appropriateness of treatment, and at the same time to give the client room to make a similar and independent judgment about the desirability of continuing to work with this particular therapist using this particular approach.

Trustworthy behavior begins during the initial telephone contact when the therapist informs the potential client about the length of sessions and the fee to be charged. Informing the client ahead of time about these things represents trustworthiness in that the client can make a more informed choice about setting up a first appointment. In addition, because it is very difficult for both clinicians and clients to make judgments about each other based on one meeting, some contextual therapists, like many other therapists, choose to adopt a procedure of using a four- to five-session trial period, describing this aspect of therapy during that first telephone call. I inform potential clients that during this period I will learn in detail about their concerns, and that I will take a detailed history from each person regarding the families they grew up in. I also mention that the "trial" period will serve to help me decide if I feel I will be able to work effectively with them, as well as giving them time to see if they are comfortable working with me. Of course it is especially important that the therapist remember to discuss this with the client at the end of the trial period. To fail to do so would seriously compromise the developing relationship.

When people inform me on the telephone that their concerns involve a spouse or partner, I always request that both people attend the first session. When I hear that the concerns involve a child, I ask that the whole family attend. I do, however, accede to parents' requests to meet with me for a first session without their children.

I have found that an effective approach to developing a "therapeutic contract" is to remind clients that we had agreed to meet for a number of initial exploratory sessions and that, these having been concluded, the time has come to decide whether or not to proceed and, if we proceed, in what fashion (number of sessions per week, etc.). If I feel that I will be able to work with clients I say this quite directly and ask them if they wish to continue to work with me. I do not regard a client's decision to stop at this point as a "premature termination," but rather as the conclusion of an extended consultation. In keeping with the goal of being trustworthy I make a particular point of avoiding the temptation of promising too much, especially with regard to how quickly results can be expected or how dramatic changes can be expected to be.

SOME PRACTICAL ISSUES

Session Attendance and Participation. Because contextual therapy is neither a traditional individual therapy nor a form of classical family therapy, questions are often raised regarding how many family members are typically seen in therapy sessions and in what combinations. The answer to these questions draws once again on the principle of multidirected partiality. The therapist's concern for all who might be affected by the therapy is paramount; decisions about which persons are actually in the therapy room are secondary. Of course, from a practical viewpoint, it is often easier to be partial to a person you have met face to face and whose history you know firsthand.

It is not crucial that all family members attend every session. It is similarly not crucial to coerce separated or divorced parents into jointly participating in therapy sessions with their children. On the other hand, every effort is made to give room to the client to consider for himself or herself whether including an estranged spouse, for example, might be in the best interests of the children. I typically do this by asking, "Would it be helpful for (missing person) to participate at some point in the future?" When working with adults some of whose concerns involve their own parents, the question may be asked about these parents. If parents have separated or divorced and the referral involves a child's well-being, my question will address the possible value of inviting the missing parent to participate. In this way the therapist has created an opportunity for the parent to gain increased constructive entitlement by making a move in the interests of his or her child. If the therapist had forced both parents to come together in order to help the children, the parents might comply but would have lost an opportunity to give spontaneously to their children.

Privacy. In this model all participants are provided opportunities for individual meetings with the therapist. Parents may wish to discuss sensitive aspects of their family histories without their children being present. Adults may also wish to talk about similar issues apart from their spouse or partner. In the section on assessment techniques I describe one way in which I talk about the option for such individual sessions with people. Unlike some forms of family therapy with which readers may be familiar, I treat material from these sessions as private, although I often encourage the individual to share certain material with others in the family. The importance of helping parents to earn constructive entitlement by giving to their children also underlies the contextual viewpoint regarding individual sessions for children and adolescents.

Developmental as well as other considerations may at times require that adolescents be provided the opportunity to talk with the therapist in private about personal concerns or matters they may not yet be prepared to face with their parents. I routinely inform both parents and adolescents that I will treat as private everything we discuss, with the exception of anything that leads me to believe that there is a risk of harm to either the young person himself or herself or to someone else. I also inform both parents and adolescents that I reserve the right to encourage the adolescent to share aspects of our "private" discussions with parents, promising that I will not do so myself without consent.

The procedure for handling privacy issues with younger children is somewhat different. Young children often have concerns they would like their parents to know about, but which they are unsure how to present. When this appears to be the case, or when a parent asks me to "see" their child alone, I block out 10 to 20 minutes at the beginning of a family session to spend alone with the child. I then utilize fairly standard techniques of individual child therapy. Having learned about those concerns that are topmost in the child's mind I typically say, "Now that I know what's been bothering you, I think your mom and dad should know too. When they come in would you like to tell them or would you like me to tell them?" Children typically ask me to tell their parents or to "help" them to talk to their parents. In the rare case when a child requests that I not tell parents about our discussion, I honor the request as long as the conditions regarding the absence of danger are met.

My motivation in conducting such individual sessions is always to help family members to improve their relationships, not to provide a substitute relationship. In my experience, when one begins to work intensively with a child on an individual basis there is always a risk of a slide into what I have referred to earlier as "unidirected partiality" - taking the child's side against the parents. This in turn carries with it the risk that a child may begin to see the "sympathetic" and "understanding" therapist as somehow a more desirable parent figure than his or her actual parent. The contextual therapist who chooses to see children and adolescents for many individual sessions should be aware of the risk of unintentionally creating a loyalty conflict.

Responses to Emergencies. There may be questions about how the contextual emphasis on exploring family resources and on facilitating family members' actions, rather than on deciding for them, affects the therapist's response to an emergency or potential emergency. In the case of a depressed and suicidal, or potentially suicidal, adolescent or adult, a contextual therapist would show the same concern for evaluating the presence of vegetative signs, degree of hopelessness, presence of a plan, and access to means of carrying out such a plan as would any other therapist. A contextual therapist who was also a clinical psychologist might use psychological tests to assess the presence of a thought disorder, the degree of impulsivity, or the presence of a learning disability. Similarly a contextual therapist with a background in psychiatry might consider prescribing an antidepressant or other medication. When presented with ongoing child abuse or neglect, a contextual therapist follows the same mandated reporting procedures required of his or her colleagues in psychology, psychiatry, or social work.

Custody Evaluations. One area in which a contextual therapist may respond differently from some other therapists is when being requested to provide expert testimony, based on working with a family as a therapist, in a child custody hearing. For the contextual therapist, beginning to work with a child and one of his or her parents automatically means being concerned for the welfare of the other parent as well as for the child and the parent who have been present in the therapy room. Multidirected partiality makes it impossible for the therapist to testify as an expert witness on behalf of either parent, regardless of whether or not they have been actively involved in treatment. This does not mean that a contextual therapist might not provide an independent evaluation in such a situation if he or she had not been involved as a therapist. In such a case, however, the contextual therapist would want to clarify the multidirected nature of the evaluation "contract."

CONTEXTUAL ASSESSMENT

The procedures used in assessing the psychological functioning of individuals, in taking individual and family histories, and in assessing family transactions and power struggles are not unique to this approach. The ways in which material gleaned from these assessments is used, however, is unique. In particular, all this information has implications for understanding fairness issues. In the following sections, in addition to considering some specific techniques for gathering information, we will be looking at the way in which this information is integrated and at its implications for understanding fairness issues.

SEQUENCE OF STEPS IN ASSESSMENT

In the next several paragraphs I will sketch out the assessment phase in a step-by-step manner as it usually occurs. The details of assessment procedures will be discussed in subsequent sections. As noted earlier, I begin with the initial telephone call, during which I explain the evaluation procedure. I begin the first session by reviewing this procedure and then asking what concerns brought the family to see me. The next step in the assessment is a brief, but crucial, one.

This step assesses the ability to acknowledge another's giving or effort to give. Inasmuch as such *acknowledgment* (a concept discussed in detail in a later section) is one sign of reliance on constructive as opposed to destructive entitlement, this procedure comprises a very valuable aspect of assessment. The technique itself is very straightforward. I have adopted the procedure of always asking the seemingly simple question, "Can you see ways in which your child (parent/spouse/sibling) has tried to be helpful to you?" I have found that it seems to work best to ask this question after the family or couple has presented their problem and before taking the family history. This procedure can be especially valuable in cases where children have been parentified or scapegoated. The simple question "Can you see ways in which your child has tried to be helpful to you?" can lead to acknowledgment of the child's giving and the beginning of a rebuilding of trustworthiness. For example, a man who had originally sought help because of what he believed to be his son's unacceptable behavior was able to acknowledge that when he was tense or worried about his work, his son would often cajole him into some athletic activity in order to help him relax.

In couple's treatment each person may be asked this question as it applies to his or her spouse. In the treatment of families with children, I ask the question as it applies to the child who is seen by the family as having a problem, whether emotional or behavioral. Asking parents questions of this sort may initially lead only to responses referring to a youngster's helpfulness with household chores. This would certainly be appropriate if it accurately reflected a child's level of giving. Symptomatic children, however, have nearly always been parentified.

Such children are often giving much more to parents than merely doing chores, typically at some developmental cost to themselves. More specifically, they may be giving a great deal to parents on the relationship dimension that has gone unacknowledged. For this reason, a contextual therapist will not be satisfied with a response limited to credit for chores. Encouraging parents to identify ways in which their children are trying to be helpful interpersonally (i.e., on the dimension of fairness) can be an important focus.

After I say something to let parents know that I can see doing chores as being helpful, I try to both assess parents' abilities to see that their children are giving more than this and encourage them to see this giving if they do not. One way to do this is to ask, "Are there other ways in which you have noticed your child trying to give to you? Have you noticed that he (or she) is particularly attentive when you are not feeling well or when something has upset you?" We will return to a detailed discussion of how these questions may be phrased in the section on "Giving Room" (pp. 56-57). A parent's ability to acknowledge this kind of interpersonal giving on the part of a child, especially a child who has, up until this time, been blamed for "bad" behavior, indicates an ability to rely on constructive entitlement and is an excellent prognostic sign.

When a couple has sought treatment the focus is placed on each person's ability to acknowledge the other person's efforts at giving. Following this brief exchange I begin asking about history as described in the section on *assessing individual and family history*. Psychological aspects of individual functioning are typically assessed on an ongoing basis, as are transactional aspects of family functioning. Historical, psychological, and transactional issues all have implications for understanding fairness issues. In subsequent sections I highlight some of these implications, reserving detailed discussions of both assessment and intervention related to fairness issues for a later section.

ASSESSING PSYCHOLOGICAL FACTORS

Contextual therapists basically assess psychological functioning in the same ways as other clinicians. A great deal of information regarding psychological functioning may be provided spontaneously during the first session, and perhaps during the initial telephone call. This is most likely to be the case when an adult seeks help for depression or anxiety, or when a parent is concerned about a child's sadness or fearfulness. Because children, especially young children, are rarely able to articulate their psychological experiences, various assessment techniques may be useful with this age group. Depending upon the presenting problem these might include telephone or face-to-face consultation with teachers or day care personnel, informal play assessment, review of school records, or psychological testing.

In the case of concerns about possible attention-deficit hyperactivity disorder or other disruptive behavior it is useful to obtain parents' and teachers' ratings using one of the instruments available for this purpose. It may also be useful to observe a child's behavior in school. As noted previously, information gleaned from the family history is often very useful in assessing psychological functioning. Some obvious examples include individuals with a family history of major depression, bipolar affective disorder, or anxiety attacks. Family history can also help in diagnosing a child's problem, as, for example, in the case of hyperactivity or a learning problem.

Clearly much of what the contextual therapist does to assess individual psychological functioning is far from unique. One way in which the assessment of individual psychology does differ from some other approaches, however, is in the way in which this information is integrated and incorporated into the assessment of issues regarding fairness in family relationships. For example, siblings, spouses, and children are all affected by the presence of significant mental illness such as schizophrenia, bipolar affective disorder, or refractory major depression in an adult family member. When I learn about the presence of such conditions I become particularly interested in the ways in which they may have affected the balance of fairness in the family. Similarly, there are fairness implications for a child who has a neurologically based learning disability or other handicapping condition.

I have emphasized the overlap between the assessment of psychological factors in this and many other therapeutic approaches. There is an important distinction to be made, however, between this and the many "family therapy" models that minimize or exclude consideration of factors related to individual psychological functioning. Here psychological differences among individuals are just as important as systemic differences between families or fairness factors within families. One psychological characteristic which I have found to be of particular value is the ability to be nondefensively self-critical. A parent or other family member's willingness to openly express concern that his or her child's or family's difficulties may be due in part to his or her actions is an excellent prognostic sign.

ASSESSING INDIVIDUAL AND FAMILY HISTORY

As in many other therapeutic approaches, assessment continues beyond what is usually referred to as the "assessment phase" into the "treatment phase." The assessment of historical issues, referred to as *existential* issues within this framework, is often largely complete by the end of the initial assessment phase, although new information about individual or family history may be learned later in treatment. Similarly, information about the psychological functioning of individual family members, especially with regard to the presence or absence of major psychopathology or significant cognitive limitations, will largely be learned before the end of the third or fourth session. Patterns of family transaction, however, may change considerably as treatment progresses and thus benefit from ongoing monitoring and reassessment. Fairness issues especially receive continued close scrutiny in every session, whether individual, marital, or family.

Unlike some family therapy approaches which emphasize the present to the exclusion of the past, a thorough personal individual and family history is extremely important in contextual therapy. My preference is to begin to obtain this history in the first session and to do so in a fairly structured manner. My standard procedure for a first session involves asking the individual, couple, or family what difficulty or concern has brought them to see me. After I have heard a response from each family member who wishes to speak, including young children, I begin to collect information about both individual and family history, recording it in the form of a genogram. Readers who are unfamiliar with the technique of drawing genograms or who are interested in learning more about their use may wish to consult McGoldrick and Gerson's (1985) book on the subject.

In introducing this phase of the assessment I simply say that in working with families I find it very helpful to learn as much as I can about the families in which people grew up. Clients find this a very reasonable and sensible explanation and cooperate willingly with the history-taking process. Children in particular seem to enjoy the process of learning more about their parents' families and often both listen attentively and participate enthusiastically. When a first session includes more than one person, and particularly when children are present, I provide an opportunity for privacy as follows:

> Parents (people) often have some aspects of their family history that they would rather discuss in private. My standard procedure is to offer individual sessions to any family member who wishes. If I ask questions you would rather not answer right now, we will have an opportunity to meet later to talk about them.

When young children are involved I take an abbreviated developmental history that is still sufficiently detailed to alert me to any problems during pregnancy, labor, infancy, or early childhood that might be affecting the child's current functioning. I continue taking the history by asking each person to tell me the names and ages of their siblings, parents, and grandparents. I ask whether parents and grandparents are living and whether they are basically healthy or have significant medical conditions. I ask about the cause of death of any deceased relative. Of course the majority of individuals have lost parents and grandparents to disease, but I have found that routinely asking the question can lead to surprising and valuable information regarding accidental deaths, suicides, and even murders.

As adults mention their brothers and sisters, I ask if they are married and have children. When individuals have been married several times or have had nonmarital relationships leading to the birth of children, I ask about these individuals and their roles in the children's lives. I typically ask people to tell me their middle names and ask if they were named for anyone in their family. It is also useful to ask about where relatives live, their current family and employment, and the nature of the relationships among them and between them and the client. In many families much of this information will be produced spontaneously if the therapist asks for the names and ages of family members and "anything else you think I should know." However the information is gathered, the therapist should try to have information spanning at least three generations. The genogram can usually be completed in the first few sessions.

Regardless of how much or how little historical information emerges in the first session, I always make sure there is time to ask a question which, like the question about giving and acknowledgment for giving, has as much to do with intervention as with assessment. The question is, "Do you see any connections between the sorts of things we have been talking about regarding your childhood and the family you grew up in and your current concerns?" I have also found that the more open-ended my question about possible connections is, the more thoughtful and relevant are my clients' responses. Asking whether their child's behavioral problems "remind" parents of anybody else is likely to bring up memories of a relative who "was always in trouble in school." A less structured question, of the sort described later under "Giving Room" (pp. 56-57), on the other hand, may lead parents to think harder and to consider more subtle and ultimately more important connections.

This process of taking individual and family histories as described up to this point is undoubtedly more similar to other approaches than it is different from them. The focus on one particular aspect of history, however, does differentiate the contextual approach from most others. I am referring here to the emphasis placed on learning about sources of destructive entitlement in the lives of all family members. As I discussed earlier, reliance on destructive entitlement can be a direct result of injustice experienced in childhood and other earlier stages of life. Acknowledgment of this injustice by those close to the person, as well as by the therapist, cannot undo the harm that occurred earlier, but it can alleviate the need to rely on the destructive entitlement. Other examples of historical information of particular interest to the contextual therapist would include instances of grown children cutting off communication with their siblings or parents, or of the exploitation of children (parentification), such as a daughter who was parentified by a mother's reliance on her for emotional support during a protracted period of marital strife.

ASSESSING FAMILY TRANSACTIONS

As I discussed in the introductory material, this dimension encompasses considerations of family structure (e.g., Minuchin, 1974); communication and interaction patterns (e.g., Watzlawick, Beavin, & Jackson, 1967; Wynne, 1965; Wynne et al., 1958); power issues (e.g., Haley, 1976); and many others reviewed by Gurman and Kniskern (1981, 1991), Levant (1984), and others.

Of the many concepts drawn from the work of these and other writers that can be helpful in contextual work are several that I have found to be particularly useful. In this and the following paragraph I am following Levant's (1984) discussion of the work of these theorists. Wynne and his colleagues' (1958) concept of the *rubber fence* as describing families that exclude any input from outside the family and which shift in ways that disallow any significant differences in perception, attitudes, or values among family members can be helpful in thinking about those families that seem to block all attempts at intervention. Wynne and his colleagues' concept of *nonmutual* versus *mutual complementarity* also has clear implications for the fairness of give and take in close relationships and is in this sense quite close to contextual thinking.

Bowen's (1966, 1978) concept of *triangulation*, particularly as used by Minuchin (1974), is particularly useful and provides a structural description of the same phenomenon I have referred to as *split loyalty*. Ackerman (1966) has used the very vivid image of the family *scapegoat* to describe a family member who is, to all appearances, rejected for being different, or for failing to adhere to family values. The following material provides a brief illustration of one commonly occurring pattern of scapegoating.

Paul: A Scapegoated Child

Ten-year-old Paul's parents requested therapy for Paul because he was "mean" to his younger sister, "disobedient and disrespectful" to his parents, and because of a persistent pattern of dishonesty. In obtaining historical information the therapist learned that several teachers had expressed concerns that it seemed very difficult for Paul to pay attention in class and that he appeared to have significant difficulties meeting expectations for reading skills. Paul's mother did not feel that these were important issues, and believed that if he would try harder he would do well. His father was concerned about the possibility that Paul might have a learning disability of some sort. They were also in constant conflict about how to respond to Paul at home. Paul's parents insisted that their relationship as a couple was without problems, and that any problems they might be having were totally due to Paul and his problems.

As Levant (1984) and others have pointed out, the scapegoat may appear to be *disloyal* while invisibly being very loyal. Many families have strong values and even prejudices which require that their children marry someone of similar cultural, ethnic, racial, and religious background. Grown children who choose to break these spoken or unspoken rules are often scapegoated, regardless of their affection and caring for their parents and their attempts to maintain good relationships with them. Ironically, in some cases these offspring may be the most loyal of children. In addition to their genuine affection and concern for their parents, these children may be keeping issues related to the family's cultural, ethnic, and religious identity alive and a focus of intense family interest in ways that might not occur otherwise.

ASSESSING FAIRNESS ISSUES

Concepts and procedures arising from the consideration of fairness in close relationships most clearly differentiate the contextual approach from many others. I have discussed the ways in which contextual therapists address the fairness implications of historical, psychological, and transactional material. Here and in the following sections on intervention we shall look more specifically and in more detail at both the ways in which fairness issues are assessed and the roles they play in interventions.

The concepts of *injustice, destructive entitlement*, and *parentification* are closely related. Because a tendency to parentify another person is one manifestation of reliance on destructive entitlement, and because destructive entitlement itself results from being subjected to injustice in one's life, these three factors are often assessed together.

Assessment of Injustice, Destructive Entitlement, and Parentification. *Injustice* occurs whenever people have been unfairly harmed in their lives. In addition to having been parentified, a person may have unfairly incurred great harm in other ways. Among these would be deprivation and loss as the result of national or international economic collapse or war, having lost a parent or both parents at an early age, or losing a child through accident or illness. Children born with physical handicaps have been unfairly harmed, as have those born with such cognitive limitations as dyslexia or even with very average ability in a family of academic superstars.

In the previous section on assessing psychological factors I briefly mentioned the fairness implications of suffering with severe mental illness or other chronic and disabling conditions. A parallel situation occurs for children who have moderate or severe learning difficulties, especially if their parents or siblings have had successful scholastic careers. In these instances I may ask a child, "Does it seem fair to you that you have to work so hard in school and have such a hard time while it is so easy for your sister?" I have found it very helpful to try to understand these and similar experiences of injustice in the lives of both children and parents in as much detail as possible. The following cases illustrate my approach to beginning to explore these issues with children and their parents.

The vignettes of Eunice and Ricky illustrate how distributive injustice resulting from having a chronic and potentially life-threatening medical condition can lead a person to rely on destructive entitlement. In Eunice's case this led to anger, disruptiveness, and suicidal threats. Ricky's father's reliance on destructive entitlement interfered with his ability to be considerate of his son's need for medical treatment; in other words, it blinded him to his son's needs. Sally's case is an example of the parentification of a child resulting from a parent's having been parentified himself to the extent that he has become blind to his child's distress. The case of Debbie illustrates the value of trying to uncover the injustice in a parent's life as a means of understanding harsh and rejecting actions toward a child. The case of Joey dramatically illustrates how an adult, severely damaged by life, can turn to, and so parentify, even a very young child. Finally, the case of Mr. S illustrates the relationship between invisible loyalty and parentification - a parent who uses his son to work through his ongoing conflicts with his own parents.

The examples include illustrations of children who have been parentified by their parents. Before presenting them I want to again stress that the adults who appear in these illustrations were children once too. In doing the actual clinical work it is at least as important, and often more important, to understand the ways in which these parents were parentified as children as it is to understand the ways in which they are now parentifying their children.

Eunice: A Case of Injustice as the
Result of Chronic Illness (Vignette #1)

Eunice was an 8-year-old girl who had been referred for treatment after engaging in escalating disruptive behavior, culminating in threats to commit suicide. In the initial session Eunice's father informed me that she suffered from brittle diabetes and that she had had multiple medical crises leading to hospitalizations. After learning about this I first asked "Does being sick and having to go to the hospital make you mad?" Eunice replied, "I hate this planet, it's not fair, and I don't want to be here." This was a clear reflection of the injustice of being so ill through no fault of her own.

Of course, the issue of unfairness is also very much present for the parent of an ill child and so I turned to Eunice's father and said, "I would think that this has to be very distressing from your side too." Eunice's father responded that he did not feel it was good for Eunice to become preoccupied by the illness and so he tended to focus more on the need for Eunice to be strong, to go to school even on days when she did not feel all that well, and generally not to give in to the illness. This response led me to think about how I might best be partial to both father and daughter as well as to the question of acknowledgment of the injustice to which both father and daughter had been subjected.

Ricky: A Father's Destructive Entitlement
Arising from a Serious Medical Condition (Vignette #1)

Ricky was an extremely hyperactive 13-year-old boy whose behavior had led to conflicts with teachers and rejection by peers. Ricky responded very well to psychostimulant medication. While receiving this medication he was more accepted by his peers and able to behave more appropriately in school. After Ricky had been taking the medication for several months, however, his father insisted that it be stopped. When this was done in accordance with his father's demands, Ricky's hyperactivity and related behavioral problems returned to their previous problematic levels.

In discussions with Ricky's father regarding his refusal to allow Ricky to receive medication, it was learned that the father was a diagnosed diabetic who refused to take insulin. Because of this he had experienced frequent hospitalizations for diabetic emergencies. Ricky's father saw his own diabetic deterioration as "inevitable" and similarly believed that Ricky just "has to get used to having a problem." From a contextual perspective, this father's experience of injustice regarding his own medical condition led to his reliance on destructive entitlement which was in turn seen in his inability to recognize the benefits of medication for his son.

The examples of injustice I listed previously refer to instances of harm due to circumstances of birth or historical factors. Some of these are examples of *distributive injustice*; the responsibility for events like war and economic depression cannot be directed at one person. The same may be said of some handicapping conditions due to prenatal or neonatal traumas. Genetically transmitted diseases are much more complex because from both the child's and parents' sides there may be elements of both distributive and specific responsibility. Consider a couple whose daughter was born with a genetically transmitted and severely handicapping condition. The mother felt that this was God's will and accepted it as such. The father, on the other hand, blamed life for doing this to him and also blamed his wife for not seeking amniocentesis as a precaution, despite the fact that she was only 23 at the time of the child's birth.

In addition to sources of injustice linked to the facts of a person's life, much injustice is experienced as the result of having been exploited by those with whom one has been in close relationships. This exploitation can take many forms but always involves the unilateral using of another person to meet one's needs. In this sense, then, the person being used is required to behave as if he or she were the selflessly giving parent of a young child. Although adults often parentify other adults, the clearest examples of such exploitation occur in families when children are *parentified* by their parents or other adults, as described in an earlier section.

Sally: Parentification as the Result of a Parent's Reliance on Destructive Entitlement

Sally, 11 years old, had been tested psychologically as the result of her parents' concerns about what they believed to be a pattern of "underachievement" in school. The psychologist felt that Sally was experiencing more internal stress than was apparent and recommended that she, her sister, and her parents participate in family therapy. Although her parents were reluctant, they followed the psychologist's recommendation. From the first session Sally appeared sad, and was noticeably less outgoing than her 12-year-old sister. After several weeks in therapy, Sally began to talk openly of her concerns and of her considerable sadness and anxiety in response to what she believed was her parents' preference for her sister.

From Sally's perspective her sister was more attractive, outgoing, athletic, and successful in school than she. In taking the family history, I learned that Sally's father had had a lonely and difficult childhood and that he had felt tremendous pressure to excel academically and to follow in his father's professional footsteps. I learned that he had had periods of depression and had been in individual therapy for several years as a youngster. After having shared this much information, the father said that he preferred not to discuss any other aspects of his childhood experiences. Near the end of the fourth session, Sally's father announced that he and his wife had decided that Sally was "really doing fine" and that therapy was no longer necessary for her or for the family. While Sally's father was explaining his thinking about this, Sally was sitting across from him crying.

In an effort to be partial to both father and daughter, I asked father, "What do you make of your daughter's crying?" He again repeated that he was sure she would "be fine." Continuing to try to be partial to him, I then asked if perhaps it was difficult to revisit issues which were so difficult for him in his own childhood. Father said that no, it wasn't, but that he preferred not to talk about them. Therapy was terminated at this point.

One view of this process might be that the parents had never really wanted treatment at all, and that it took them 4 weeks to act. Within the framework I am presenting here, however, the father's apparent insensitivity to his daughter's distress was most remarkable. What had happened? To the extent that the father had been used to add to his parents' good feelings about themselves at having produced a "genius," he had been parentified in his own childhood. His childhood experience in individual therapy, although it may have helped with his depression, may also have led to a building up of destructive entitlement, perhaps because he was the only family member singled out (i.e., scapegoated) as "needing help."

Perhaps the father felt that once as a "patient" was enough, that he would not, could not, go through the process again. And, following this line of thinking, perhaps the father's reliance on his destructive entitlement made it impossible for him to see his daughter's distress and equally impossible for him to take action to help her at that moment. In this sense then, he had parentified his daughter, placing her psychological needs second to his. In addition, it appeared as if she had been parentified just as he had, by being put under pressure to perform, to match her sister's level of accomplishment, and to gratify her parent's wishes. In addition, Sally's depression suggests that she had been unable to find ways to give to her parents on her own terms, as opposed to those set up by her grandparents for her father and by her parents for her - that is, academic success.

If Sally's father had been able to rely more on constructive entitlement he might have been able to go through the difficult therapy process in order to help his daughter. In this case one of my early goals would have been to help Sally's parents to provide opportunities for her to give to them, and to help them acknowledge the ways in which she had been giving.

The next cases illustrate how looking for injustice in a parent's life can be application of multidirected partiality. They also clearly illustrate how harm that befalls a parent can lead to reliance on destructive entitlement and so to the destructive parentification of children.

Debbie: Injustice Leading to
Reliance on Destructive Entitlement
and Parentification (Vignette #1)

Debbie was an 11-year-old girl whose mother frequently threatened to have a state agency remove her from the home and place her in foster care. There was nothing apparent in Debbie's behavior that would have warranted such harsh actions. In therapy sessions Ms. G made statements such as, "After you're in a foster home you'll realize how good you've had it here. After you've been beaten or sexually abused in a foster home, you'll appreciate how much I've done for you."

Such statements may at first seem to show simple cruelty. Further exploration of Ms. G's history, however, told another story. Ms. G herself had been one of many children in her family, all of whom had been placed in foster care by their mother. Ms. G's own mother, in turn, had been one of nine children, all of whom had grown up in foster care. In attempting to assess the extent of Ms. G's destructive entitlement, the therapist asked Ms. G if she felt that Debbie had had a better life than she had herself. Ms. G responded that Debbie had already benefited by being in a relatively stable home for over 11 years, a longer period of stability than Ms. G had ever experienced in her own childhood.

Joey: Extreme Destructive Parentification (Vignette #2)

A later session with Joey, whose case was first described as an illustration of the right to give, is illustrative of parentification in an extreme form. After 9 months of treatment, Joey's mother, stabilized on antipsychotic medication, began to attend therapy sessions. In one of these sessions she asked Joey, "Do you love me, baby?" When Joey responded that he did and gave his mother a hug, Joey's mother asked the follow-up question, "Very much?"

Later in the same session, Joey's mother reflected about the time when she repeatedly stabbed her son in the chest, "When you said, 'Mommy I'm dying,' that's when I stopped." Near the end of this session the therapist noticed Joey using a toy stethoscope to listen to his mother's heart and asked, "Is mommy sick?" Joey answered that his mother was sick and that he was the only one who could make her better. In this case one can only speculate about the nature of the unfairness in early life (environmental, familial, or biological) that may have led to Joey's mother's illness and to her subsequent parentification of her son.

Mr. S: Parentification and Invisible Loyalty

A man who had cut himself off from his parents and who frequently described them as "authoritarian and punitive" found himself in frequent conflicts with his teenage son. These conflicts typically escalated rapidly when the father felt his son was being irresponsible or disrespectful, behaviors his parents would have found intolerable. The therapist identified the pattern of conflict with his son as a manifestation of invisible loyalty and so tried to help the father learn about his parents' backgrounds so that he might come to accept them with their faults and to reconnect with them. The goal here was the achievement of visible loyalty through exoneration.

INTERVENTION PROCEDURES

ASSESSING FAIRNESS ISSUES
LEADS DIRECTLY TO INTERVENTION

I commented earlier that the assessment of fairness issues blends in a seamless manner into intervention procedures that aim to help people enhance their capacities for considerate relating. These procedures help people move away from a focus on pathology and toward a focus on resources; away from a focus on blaming and toward a focus on crediting. Multidirected partiality is central to intervention, just as it is to assessment. Interventions designed to heighten fairness issues also include crediting, helping people to acknowledge each other's giving, giving room, and lending weight. The next vignette illustrates this blending of assessment into intervention in an initial session with a family who had requested help because of their child's disruptive behaviors. The vignette shows how parents can rely on constructive entitlement despite having accumulated a great deal of destructive entitlement. It also shows the dramatic changes that can occur when attention is drawn to the ways in which a previously blamed child is trying to give to his or her parents. Focusing on questions of giving and receiving, instead of the expected detailed interviewing regarding the "bad" behavior that has brought the family to therapy, often begins to draw the family's interest toward questions of fairness and away from blame.

The M Family: Initial Session

When Tim, a 10-year-old boy with moderate developmental delay, was brought to the clinic by his mother and father, they stated that he was "totally out of control," that he refused to do anything for himself to the extent of refusing to wake up, to shower, or to dress himself, and that he had frequent temper tantrums. He had told his parents that he hated them and himself. He had broken household objects as well as some of his toys. He had said that no one loved him and that he wished he were dead. Tim's parents felt that they had exhausted all their emotional reserves and that he was totally unmanageable. They

39

requested that he be considered for placement in residential treatment.

Both parents were visibly frustrated and angry during the family interview. My question about ways in which Tim might have shown that he would like to be helpful surprised his parents, because they expected that I would focus on his inappropriate and disruptive behaviors. This basic contextual assessment and intervention technique is described in the section on "Sequence of Steps in Assessment" (pp. 24-26). Both parents, however, were able to credit Tim as having a tender side and as being particularly aware of both his mother's and father's feelings.

Perhaps the most telling moment in this interview came after I asked Tim if he would like to do more, if he would feel better about himself if he got himself up in the morning. Tim said that yes, that he would like to do more for himself. I then asked mother and father, "Does it seem this way to you too? Does it seem that Tim would like to do more, if he knew what to do?" Despite their still-smoldering anger, Tim's parents said that they thought this might be true.

I was impressed by the ability of these parents to seriously consider the possibility that their son might want to behave differently, and that he might be able to do so with some help. This ability to see their child's side, indicative of reliance on constructive entitlement, led me to feel positively about the prognosis for this case.

ANGER AND DISRUPTIVE BEHAVIORS IN CHILDREN

This case is representative of a large number of cases in which the initial concern focuses on a child whose behavior is a source of distress to his or her parents, teachers, and other adults. As is well known, the greatest number of referrals for therapy for children, especially in clinics, occur because a child has engaged in behaviors that disturb others much more than they disturb the child himself or herself. From a diagnostic perspective these problems include attention-deficit hyperactivity disorder, oppositional defiant disorder, and conduct disorder, and are typically referred to as disruptive behavior disorders. These disorders are currently receiving much attention from researchers, much of which focuses on possible neurological, neurochemical, and genetic causal factors. Some researchers believe that most, if not all, youngsters who have difficulty following rules and appropriately controlling their behavior suffer from neurological dysfunction. Other investigators suggest that this may be true only for the most disruptive subgroup of these children. Whatever the final outcome of these studies, one thing seems clear. Most of these children, whatever their neurological status finally turns out to be, both experience and show very significant problems with anger. From the perspective offered here, a youngster's anger and disruptive behavior indicate an imbalance between what the child gives to others and what he or she receives from others. These are often signs that the child has experienced, or is currently experiencing, great unfairness. This unfairness leads to an increase in destructive entitlement, reliance on which can be seen in a youngster's apparent insensitivity to the way in which his or her behavior impacts on others. Of course, adults are just as likely to rely on destructive entitlement resulting from injustice experienced in their lives (Goldenthal, 1992).

In some cases this unfairness may be of the sort for which no one person or even group of persons may be held responsible. This is distributive injustice in that the blame must be distributed over all of life and not assigned to anyone in particular. The unfairness of a youngster suffering from a chronic life-threatening illness, for example, or of a child losing a parent due to an accident or illness, would fall into this category. Other instances of distributive injustice would include having a significant neurologically based problem which interferes with development, particularly with scholastic achievement. In many cases, however, the unfairness, and thus the source of anger, is destructive parentification and not the learning problem itself. A child with a learning problem, whether it is a specific learning disability or an attentional difficulty which interferes with school work, may be unfairly compared to siblings, may be blamed, or may even be infantilized to the point of being discouraged from trying to achieve at all.

In the case of a serious chronic illness, the parentification may take the form of parental denial of the unfairness inherent in having such an illness. Children may then be put in a situation of assuming responsibility for their parents' feelings. Expressing their own feelings regarding the unfairness of having the illness may be upsetting to their parents, and so becomes taboo. The failure to recognize a child's developmental needs is itself a sign of the adult's reliance on destructive entitlement and a signal to look for the unfairness in that adult's earlier life.

Excerpts from later sessions with the M family illustrate how contextual principles and techniques are used in working with a family whose child has been brought for treatment as the direct result of engaging in disruptive behaviors. These excerpts and session summaries emphasize the use of multidirected partiality. They also contain examples of crediting, giving room, and especially the ways in which a therapist can help parents to acknowledge the ways their child may be trying to be helpful, as discussed in the earlier section outlining the sequence of steps in contextual assessment.

The M Family: Later Sessions

Session 2. This session began with Tim's father recounting a recent incident in a shopping center in which Tim had had a dramatic temper tantrum, including, "lying on his back kicking and screaming" because he had thought that he would not be allowed to buy a toy or to choose which running shoes would be purchased for him. After listening to this story, I was explicitly partial to Tim.

PG: What is your side of the story, Tim? When something like this happens, everyone has their own story to tell. I'd like to hear your story about what happened in the store. It might be the same as Dad's or it might be different.

Tim: I asked for a toy. Dad said "No" . . . I had a fit.

PG: (Speaking to Tim's parents) Do you think that a fit might be a way of trying to say something, maybe not the best way, but still a way of saying, "I'm angry" or "I'm upset"? (Turning to Tim) Tim, when you are upset is it difficult for you to put your feelings into words? Or can you do that?

Tim: No, can't do that.

Here my goal was simply to continue to be partial to Tim by highlighting the way in which his language difficulties might lead to temper tantrums and other disruptive behaviors due to frustration about not being able to express himself. In this same session I began to explore sources of injustice in his mother's life by talking with her about her childhood and young adulthood. I learned that her life had been marked by a number of losses. Her father had died when she was young, and her brother had died in a freak auto accident.

Session 3. This session continued the focus on exploring injustice in Ms. M's life. She talked about her brother, whose birthday would have been this week, and whom she missed deeply. She also spoke of her very difficult relationship with her own mother whom she described as extremely critical and at times verbally and even physically abusive.

Session 4. In this session we returned to the question of Tim's wish to do more for himself, specifically to get himself up in the morning. I also made a point of addressing the inherent loyalty issue which emerges whenever a person speaks critically of a family member to a nonfamily member, in this case the therapist: "Last week you talked about a lot of very personal and family concerns. I wonder if you regret anything that you may have said?" In this session we began to explore Mr. M's early life, especially his family life as a child. He was disturbed by Tim's restlessness, and criticized Tim for this. The interchange which followed provides another example of the use of multidirected partiality as well as the resource orientation which is central to this approach. In the next excerpt I suggest that what may appear to be impolite behavior on Tim's part may actually reflect his interest in his father's history.

Father: Let me ask you a question, Tim. When your mom was talking to the doctor, you were nice and quiet. How come you have to make comments in the background when I'm talking?
PG: I think that's a good question. Because on the one hand, you might say Tim's being impolite or something.
Father: Yeah, impolite.
PG: Impolite. On the other hand, something occurred to me. I don't know if you would see it this way, but perhaps he's especially interested in the story of your childhood. He's a boy, you were a boy. Similar. . . .
Father: Very similar.

Later in this session Tim's mother introduced her feeling that Tim was growing up too rapidly. I discussed this with her, trying to be partial to her need for closeness with her son, while helping her to see opportunities to give to him by helping him to be more independent.

Mother: I was saying to my husband the other night, "We might as well enjoy his young years while we can because before we turn around he'll be a teenager and wanting to be off with his friends."
PG: It's hard to watch him grow up so fast.
Mother: Yeah.
PG: Last time you mentioned that you had considered giving Tim an alarm clock so that he could wake up by himself, but that you hadn't done it yet.
Mother: Mmmm mmmm.
PG: Perhaps your hope that Tim would get himself up in the morning is only one side; that if he had an alarm clock it would be easier for you.
Mother: Yeah.
PG: But, maybe there's a feeling of loss, too.
Mother: Uh huh.
PG: If he doesn't need you for that anymore.
Mother: Yeah. He does some things on his own. Yeah, that hurts me, you know, that bothers me some. You know, I think, yeah, this is my little boy growing up. I guess, you know, all mothers feel that way.
PG: I think so.
Mother: It's a different bond between a mother and a daughter. Mother and daughter, yeah. But a mother and a son, it's more clingy. You don't want your little boy to grow up.
PG: You mean you're clinging to him.
Mother: Yeah.

The preceding exchange illustrates two facets of my partiality to Tim's mother. First, I acknowledged how it can hurt parents when children begin to grow up and need them less. The second example of my partiality in this section occurred when I directly clarified Ms. M's own statement that she is clinging to her son and not vice versa. Drawing her attention to the possibility that she may be using Tim in response to her own needs illustrates the way that a therapist may be partial by helping someone to face a difficult aspect of their own feelings and behavior. Mother's self-understanding is illustrative of her capacity for considerate giving, in other words, of her reliance on constructive entitlement.

Mother: Mmmm hmmm. I, you know, I look at him, and I think, God, he'll be 10 in 2 months.
PG: He's almost 10.
Mother: And . . . but, I'm thinkin', when you really see a boy grow. And you know they're getting older. And you know he ain't my little boy no more.
PG: When Tim was a little baby he needed you to give to him. And all he could do was take it in. Now, maybe, he needs to be able to give to you in some way.

At this point the issue of a child's right to give becomes important. I try to be partial to Tim's mother and her need to give to Tim while suggesting that it will be helpful if she can provide opportunities for him to give to her and his father.

Mother: Mmmm mmmm.
PG: (Speaking to Tim) It seems to me that you like to give things to your mom and dad.
Tim: Uh huh.
PG: (To Ms. M) So maybe that's what using the alarm clock is all about.
Mother: Mmmm mmmm. I know I gotta. He's gettin' older. I want him to be independent, like I was.

Session 5. This session focused largely on Tim's wish to be helpful to his mother, for example, by getting himself up and ready for school.

Session 6. This session focused on Ms. M's feelings about her mother whom she described as a "mean, evil woman." I tried to interest Ms. M in learning more about her mother's childhood and background as a step toward exoneration.

Session 7. Ms. M tried to "straighten things out" with her mother on the telephone during the past week. Ms. M also provided information about her mother's history of emotional problems and her current refusal to accept suggestions that she seek professional help.

Session 8. Mr. and Ms. M reported significant improvement in Tim's behavior during a brief telephone conversation. Much of the improvement seemed to reflect their increased ability to see Tim as trying to please them rather than as being a "bad boy."

Session 9. Ms. M had a number of significant health concerns which were the focus of this session. Tim was noticeably fidgety as these issues were being discussed. Because of her understandable preoccupation with her own physical well-being, Ms. M was not initially able to see her son's fidgetiness as reflecting his concern about her health, instead assuming he was just being disruptive. Using a technique similar to that illustrated in the excerpts from earlier sessions, I acknowledged her distress while trying to highlight the possibility that Tim was concerned about her and unable to express it verbally, leading to his fidgetiness.

Session 10. Tim's parents reported that there had been significant improvements. They began to express their feeling that things were going so well that regular therapy sessions would no longer be necessary. I made it clear that they could call to make an appointment at any time in the future when they felt additional sessions would be helpful, either for issues related to Tim or for other issues. Ms. M called later in the year and asked for an appointment for herself to talk about the relationship between her and her mother.

Anger, depression, and disturbances of conduct frequently co-occur in youngsters, especially during adolescence. At times these problems can be accompanied by suicidal ideation. The next case illustrates just such a confluence of factors.

Roberta: Anger, Depression, and Substance Abuse in Adolescence

Roberta was a 14-year-old girl whose single-parent mother had had a difficult history marked by maternal abandonment, unhappy experiences in foster care, and two failed marriages. Although Roberta's mother had abused drugs as an adolescent and a young woman, she had not had this problem since Roberta was very young. She had, however, been distracted and overwhelmed by life's responsibilities, and had consequently been inconsistent in parenting her daughter. At the time of referral, Roberta was failing in school despite above-average abilities and in addition had begun to drink, smoke marijuana regularly, and experiment with various other drugs. When pressed, Roberta acknowledged that she felt depressed at times and that she had thought about suicide.

Roberta's mother was at a loss about what to do. She feared that Roberta might go through the same difficult times that she had experienced as a young person; and yet, having had no model of reliable parenting, she was unsure of how to respond to Roberta. The mother's own destructive entitlement was a further complicating factor. As a direct result of the injustice experienced in her early life, she had been unable to recognize Roberta's developmental needs. She tended to rely on Roberta for solace during times of loneliness, unwittingly parentifying her. At times she was overly lenient and laissez-faire, at other times harsh and punitive.

Within this framework Roberta's depression can be seen as reflecting her inability to earn entitlement and a sense of self-worth through giving appropriately to her mother. The parentification involved in taking care of her mother's emotional needs was reflected in the anger she directed toward her mother, but this had done nothing to enhance her own self-worth. Cotroneo and Krasner (1976) have suggested that turning toward drugs can be understood as a wish for a reliable parent and as a reliance on the drug in the place of a parent.

Here, as in the earlier cases, the principle of multidirected partiality provided the primary guideline during all stages of therapy. The therapist explored the mother's history, learning of her difficult past and the manner in which her destructive entitlement had roots in the injustice of her own childhood and adolescence. In exploring Roberta's side, the therapist asked if she saw her mother's wish that she get off drugs and do well in school as a reflection of caring or just a desire to control her. Roberta's response that she did see the caring aspect of her mother's behavior further suggested that Roberta was, through her apparent rebellious behavior, seeking to spur her mother into a more reliable stance as a parent and into exerting more consistent parental control. The issue of reliable parenting, and Roberta's need for this, continued to be a major focus of therapy in this case.

The therapist aimed to help both mother and daughter with this issue by continuing to be partial to both of them: to the daughter's anger and resentment for past neglect, and to the mother's confusion, anxiety, and uncertainty about how to be an effective parent. Intertwined with these issues was also the significant question of invisible loyalty. Roberta appeared to be disloyal to her mother by openly flaunting her rejection of her mother's values regarding schoolwork and drug use. But beneath the surface, the question remained as to whether Roberta was being invisibly loyal by replicating her mother's early life.

Some intervention procedures have been anticipated in the discussion of assessment, especially the assessment of factors related to relational fairness (e.g., loyalty and split loyalty, learning about past injustice, reliance on constructive versus destructive entitlement, parentification, and the ability to acknowledge others' giving). All contextual intervention procedures apply the principle of multidirected partiality, trying to see an issue as it is seen by each person involved. Because it is impossible to achieve this in any absolute sense, the operative principle then becomes that of working hard to see the sides of all those people who are likely to be affected by the outcome of the therapy.

MULTIDIRECTED PARTIALITY VERSUS IMPARTIALITY

An impartial therapeutic stance prescribes neutrality and proscribes ever taking anyone's side. A multidirected stance permits and even encourages taking sides, but requires the therapist to try to take all sides equally. The next case illustrates the use of this principle in a particularly difficult case of split loyalty. It also illustrates the way in which a therapist can lend his or her weight to one person or another, a technique discussed in more detail in a later section.

Kerry: Multidirected Partiality and Split Loyalty

Nine-year-old Kerry's mother informed the therapist that her son was unmanageable, oppositional, and defiant. In family therapy sessions, Kerry frequently yelled at his mother, said that he did not care if she was alive or dead, said that he did not want her to love him, and said that he would like to be adopted or placed in a foster home. Kerry became very upset whenever the name of his father, from whom his mother had been divorced, was mentioned in sessions. The divorce had been difficult and there was a great deal of ill feeling between the parents. At these times Kerry typically protested that his mother was "always blaming" his father and "saying bad things about him."

Prior to beginning treatment, Kerry had lived in his father's home and had told his mother that his father had physically abused him, leading to his being moved to his mother's home. At this time Kerry's behavior had become so problematic that his mother had begun to consider the option of foster placement. The therapist asked Kerry if his mother would be upset if he lived with his father and vice versa. Kerry somewhat sullenly agreed that this was the case.

The therapist asked Kerry's mother, "Do you think that Kerry's harsh statements about you and about living in a foster home might be his way of trying to solve the problem of not upsetting either one of you by choosing to live with the other?" The therapist then mused, as if to himself, "You know, Kerry screams and yells so much about hating you (mother), but it seems to me that he cares a great deal about your feelings."

The therapist's attempts to be partial to Kerry are evident in bringing the split loyalty issue to the surface. His statement about the strong caring underlying Kerry's verbal aggression represented an effort to be partial to both mother and son.

The A Family: Partiality to Divorced Parents

A therapist was consulted by a woman who had separated from her husband and was concerned about her child's very poor school performance. The therapist worked at seeing her side, including her criticisms of her estranged husband. The therapist also worked to see the child's side, which was dominated by conflicting loyalties to his mother and father. In addition to being partial to the mother and son, however, the therapist tried to be partial to the side of the absent father by consistently encouraging the mother to invite the father to attend a session either with her or by himself, and by speaking positively of the father to both the child and mother. The therapist was also partial to all sides by explaining to the mother that if he were to be required to testify in a custody proceeding, he would only encourage the court to insure that both parents had freedom to maintain their relationships with their son.

The B Family: Multidirected
Partiality in a Case of Parental Separation

Ten-year-old William's father and mother had been separated for nearly a year and were in the midst of divorce proceedings when William was brought to the clinic by his mother. Much of William's difficulty seemed to be linked to the presence of split loyalty brought on by the very high degree of mistrust between his parents. In order to avoid contributing further to this split loyalty and to be partial to Mr. B's side, the thera-

pist suggested that William's mother invite his father to participate in therapy sessions. When the therapist was informed that
Mr. B's lawyer had strongly discouraged this, the father was in-
vited to talk with the therapist on the telephone regarding his
concerns about his son. This not being possible either, the therapist, operating on the principle of multidirected partiality,
sought to raise the father's side whenever opportunities arose
during the therapy sessions. When William complained that his
father never did anything interesting with him during weekend
visits, the therapist suggested the possibility that his father
might welcome suggestions from William himself, and that
perhaps he had planned activities that he thought William
would enjoy.

From a contextual perspective, any marital conflict serious
enough to warrant treatment has implications for the couple's
children. As discussed in an earlier section, severe marital conflict and mistrust between parents can lead to a situation of split
loyalty for children, an existential dilemma with very serious psychological consequences. Following is an example of contextual
therapy procedures applied to a case of split loyalty.

The C Family: Severe
Marital Discord and Split Loyalty

Billy and Tommy, 6-year-old twins, were initially brought
to the clinic by their mother, who expressed concerns that both
children seemed very upset upon returning from visits with
their father, and that they often were enuretic for 2 or 3 days
following such visits. Ms. C asked if the children should be
seeing their father at all. She also talked about how it upset her
that her parents took her estranged husband's side in the various
conflicts that had arisen since their separation. In order to be
partial to Ms. C, as well as to understand the family context of
these difficulties, a detailed history was taken in the first session and recorded in the form of a genogram. Knowing of her
experiences, the therapist was able to credit Ms. C for experiencing the injustice of having her own mother turn against her
at a time when her support was needed.

The principle of multidirected partiality led the therapist to
consider Mr. C's side as well. To this end, Ms. C was asked if
she thought it might be helpful to have one or more joint ses-

sions with her husband, a suggestion she followed. It is worth noting that the therapist did not insist, because to require a joint session for which one or both persons were not at least reasonably prepared would be likely to exacerbate the split loyalty. Giving Ms. C room to choose to have the therapist hear her husband's side of the story, however, gave her an opportunity to earn constructive entitlement by considering her children's father's perspective.

The initial joint session focused on obtaining a detailed history from Mr. C which was also recorded in genogram format. Mr. C was very critical of his wife's lifestyle, characterizing her as irresponsible, emotionally unstable, and prone to rage against him and the children when under stress. Ms. C, as would be expected, defended herself, and criticized Mr. C for speaking ill of her to the children and for trying to keep her mother and brother on his side. In situations of this sort, it is obviously pointless to try to figure out who is right and who is wrong. These are also situations in which the resource orientation of contextual therapy, along with the principle of multidirected partiality, can be most helpful.

Following these principles, the therapist sought to discover ways to begin to restore trust between the parents. Mr. C was asked whether, if he knew of some way to help his wife care for the children, he would want to do so. He was also asked whether he could see it as potentially troubling to the children to hear their grandmother denigrate their mother. Ms. C was asked whether, in addition to the obvious criticisms, it seemed possible that some of her husband's statements reflected genuine concern for the children. By trying to see all sides, the therapist tried to help each parent see the side of the other.

UNCOVERING RESOURCES

Beginning with the initial session and continuing throughout therapy, the contextual therapist is much more interested in searching for *resources* than in uncovering pathology. Uncovering family resources that can increase *trustworthiness* and facilitate achieving a fair balance of give and take in the family can take several forms. In many settings, especially public agencies and clinics, we often speak of "resources" with reference to support services another agency may offer, or perhaps to family members who may provide housing, childcare, or refuge from an unpleasant or dangerous situation. In this model, however, *resources* are available means for considerate giving and receiving. The operant question is whether family members have the potential to consider the fairness of their own and other's needs to a greater extent than they have done thus far.

To the extent that people have the potential to rely more on constructive entitlement in their family relationships and so to consider each other's needs, there are untapped resources for giving and receiving. The concept of *trustworthiness* also has a specific meaning within this framework. One's trustworthiness depends on one's ability to modify both one's demands for receiving and one's willingness to give to the other based on consideration of fairness.

ACKNOWLEDGMENT

Trustworthiness increases when one person is able to acknowledge the giving of another. Questions asked during the assessment phase regarding giving and acknowledgment for giving are also interventions which are designed to draw people's attention to this aspect of their relationships. There are two forms of acknowledgment, both of which involve giving credit to another person. The first involves giving credit to another person for considerate actions. For example, a child takes his mother's hand when he sees that she is tearful while talking about her recent divorce. The child's mother may then acknowledge this caring, thanking her child for being supportive. The second involves acknowledging the injustice (unfairness) that has occurred in someone else's life. Examples would include acknowledging how one's actions have harmed another, and acknowledging the unfairness of having been born with a disability or chronic life-threatening illness. Acknowledging that another has been harmed is one indicator of one's ability to act based on constructive rather than destructive entitlement.

Some forms of giving are much less obvious and may require clarification from the therapist before family members are able to give credit. In the midst of a family session, a 9-year-old boy complains that his parents are "always fighting about where to live and what kind of house to buy." The parents' initial reaction may be anger, but when they can see his statements as reflecting his desire to help them resolve a problem by making it a focus of therapy, they may be able to credit his words and his caring.

Joseph: Acknowledgment
of a Child's Giving to His Parent

Joseph, a 12-year-old boy, had been having trouble in school for failure to follow rules as well as for failing to complete his homework. In a family session, Joseph's parents, who were angry about his behavior, were asked if, despite the school difficulties, there were ways in which Joseph had shown his desire to be helpful to them. At this point Joseph's mother, slightly tearful, reached to place her hand gently on her son's in acknowledgment of his concerns for her in her grief over the death of her father.

Kevin: Multidirected Partiality and
Acknowledgment of a
Child's Concern for an Ill Parent

Kevin was a 12-year-old boy whose father had recently been diagnosed as diabetic. In a family session the discussion focused on the father's intense anger at Kevin for an infraction of a household rule. Kevin commented that perhaps his father's outbursts were partially due to fatigue and low blood sugar resulting from his diabetes. Both his father and mother initially were further angered by Kevin's remarks, feeling that he was trying to distract them and the therapist from the business at hand. The therapist's response illustrates the technique of using multidirected partiality to foster acknowledgment. It also illustrates the use of open-ended questioning, which gives parents room to see their children's side and so to earn entitlement in their children's eyes.

This technique involves turning to the other family members present and inviting them to see the possible merit in what they initially took as a totally negative comment. In this instance, the therapist mused, as if thinking aloud, "Well, I suppose that on one hand it may seem that Kevin is being sort of impudent, and of course that's a natural part of being a teenager. On the other hand, though, I wonder if it is possible that Kevin is actually concerned about his father's health and is trying to be helpful?" After some thought, Kevin's mother, and later his father, were able to credit him for his caring and efforts to be helpful.

Bobby: Acknowledgment
of Giving Between Siblings

Bobby had been diagnosed as hyperactive, oppositional, and defiant. He was repeating the 5th grade after a failure the previous year, and had recently been suspended for fighting. His older brother, Alvin, a 7th grader, had also experienced school difficulties and had been suspended for fighting. In a family session, Alvin expressed concerns that Bobby had been doing worse in school and that his behavior was growing more uncontrollable than it had been in the past. Hearing this, and wishing to highlight family resources rather than family pathology, the therapist asked their mother, "Does it sound to you like Alvin is concerned about Bobby and wants to help him?" The boys' mother agreed and acknowledged that despite Alvin's fighting, of which she disapproved strongly, he did seem to be trying to help his younger brother.

It has been my experience that, when given room to consider a child's caring and giving, even parents who have had very difficult lives themselves can often give credit and acknowledge their children's attempts to help them. Giving to others without acknowledgment often leads to anger, resentment, and, in the case of children and adolescents, aggressive acting out. I have frequently seen dramatic reductions in anger, verbal aggression, and defiance in children following an increase in their parent's abilities to acknowledge the children's giving.

Just as one person can acknowledge another's giving, so can one acknowledge one's own failures to give and to consider another's or one's own parentification of a child. This kind of acknowledgment partially immunizes the child against the destructive effects of being parentified. The child may still be giving out of proportion to his or her age and position in the family, but the acknowledgment of the giving can soften the accumulation of destructive entitlement and militate against future reliance on the inevitable destructive entitlement. The next cases illustrate this aspect of acknowledgment.

Albert: Acknowledgment
of Caretaking Behavior

Albert was a 6-year-old boy whose mother complained that he refused to do as he was told, went where and when he pleased, and was rude and generally oppositional. After listening to her complaints I said, "I can certainly see that it would be very distressing to have Albert talk back constantly and I agree that he should learn to be more respectful. I wonder, though, if you can see some areas in which he tries to be helpful to you." Albert's mother replied that she had noticed that Albert liked to help with the dishes.

I commented that this sounded like a good thing, and asked, "Are there some ways in which you have noticed Albert trying to give to you as one person to another, not just in doing chores?" Albert's mother seemed at a loss momentarily. At this point I noticed that Albert had picked up the stethoscope from a toy doctor's kit and was pretending to listen to his mother's heart and chest. I told her that I had noticed this and then asked, "Does Albert seem particularly interested in your health? Does he show caring when you don't feel well, for example?" Mother then said that he did seem to try to be especially nice when she was ill, and that he often watched his 2-year-old brother when she took her naps in the afternoon.

Eunice: Acknowledgment of Unfairness (Vignette #2)

In the first vignette describing this case it may have initially appeared that Eunice's father was unable to acknowledge the unfairness of Eunice's condition. I suggested an individual session so that he and I could discuss his history and his side of his daughter's illness. Within the framework presented here, I chose this option as a way of being partial to him and in order to maximize the possibility of learning about injustice he had incurred in his life.

Through taking the family history I learned that Eunice's father's parents and brother had all died at relatively young ages and that he had been the primary caregiver for all of them. I also learned that he feared that he carried the genetic trait responsible for his daughter's diabetes. Even though none of the deceased relatives had been diabetic, he felt responsible for and guilty about his daughter's condition. I also learned that although he believed he demanded a lot from Eunice, he often had difficulty setting clear limits on her behavior and on following through with consequences when she failed to adhere to his rules for acceptable behavior.

In these sessions I asked him if his worry about Eunice and his guilt sometimes made it hard for him to insist on compliance or to deny any of her requests for special favors. He agreed that this was the case. As we continued to meet both alone and with Eunice, he grew more comfortable in his resolve to insist on appropriate behavior while simultaneously being freer to readily acknowledge the unfairness of Eunice's illness.

GIVING ROOM

I try to provide opportunities for all family members to earn credit and to build up constructive entitlement by considerate giving. To the extent that I give directly to their children, for example, I may inadvertently deprive parents of the opportunity of giving. If I acknowledge the children's efforts instead of inviting their parents to do so, then the parents' acknowledgment might seem a weak echo of my acknowledgment. Similarly, if I push people to give to each other, I may unwittingly denigrate the resultant giving in the eyes of the recipient. And so my goal is to draw people's attention to opportunities for considerate giving of which they were previously unaware, thus giving them room for spontaneously expanding the resources for giving and receiving in the family.

Jack: Giving Room in a
Case of Subtle Parentification

Jack was a 10-year-old boy who, at the time of referral, lived with his father and stepmother, his parents having divorced when he was 6. Due to the requirements of his job, Jack's father left for work before Jack caught the school bus. There had been frequent arguments in the mornings, for example over whether or not Jack had completed his homework or had dressed properly for school. Jack was sensitive to these arguments and frequently telephoned his father at work from home before he left for school to say hello and "make up." In a therapy session, Jack asked "How come I always have to be the one to call first and apologize?"

This pattern illustrates the way in which even a well-intentioned and caring parent can fail to see his or her child's developmental needs. The inability to see such needs, especially when the result is a situation in which a child must become parent to the parent, comprises the essence of reliance on destructive parentification.

The therapist's first goal was to give room for Jack's father to see Jack's side. The therapist felt that if he told Jack's father directly that he should behave differently he would rob the father of the option of giving to his son in this way. And so he particularly wanted to use an open-ended questioning approach, to give Jack's father room to earn merit through consideration of Jack's needs. The therapist's first step was to ask, "Is there merit to what Jack is saying; is there something to it?" Jack's father answered that there did indeed seem to be something to Jack's complaint, that it did not seem fair that the burden of apology should always rest with his son.

Because Jack's father's level of destructive entitlement was moderate he was immediately able to see that his son was distressed over the repetitive situation. As soon as he became aware of Jack's discomfort, he began to work to change. The refractory nature of parentification, however, was evident in his turning to his child to ask that he remind him (father) to call him if that is what he wishes. This request, of course, led to further leading questioning by the therapist.

Some people, like Jack's father, are able to respond in this way to the most open-ended of questions. Similar responses sometimes occur when parents are asked in a first session to point to ways in which their children try to give to them. In the majority of clinical situations, however, open-ended, albeit leading, questions of this sort do not provide enough structure for the people with whom we work. In these cases it becomes necessary to gradually provide more and more structure, in a sense to lead people more directly.

THE FUNNEL: A MODEL FOR TIMING INTERVENTIONS

An image I have found helpful in narrowing the focus of questions, and of providing structure while still leaving room for people to respond as they choose, is that of the funnel. A funnel starts out wide and gradually narrows, eventually constraining the fluid it contains to a very narrow path. This image of a funnel can readily be applied to the use of leading questions which are intended to draw people's interest and attention to issues of fairness. Applying the model, the therapist begins by asking the most open-ended and vague questions imaginable. I have already presented some examples of these: "Do you see any connections between the sorts of things we have been talking about in the family you grew up in and your current concerns?" and "Can you point to areas in which you have been able to notice that your child tries to give to you?"

The next step in narrowing the funnel is to provide more specific guidelines, perhaps including some concrete examples. With regard to acknowledging a child's giving, questions such as "Does he (she) seem to notice when you don't feel well, or when you are a bit down or worried?" fit into this category. Once beyond the assessment phase, the therapist may wish to continue to narrow in, eventually making a bald statement such as "I don't know if you would see it the way that I do, but it seems to me that your son (daughter) really cares and wants to give to you." Couching this observation even a little bit tentatively still leaves some room for parents to give without appearing slavish.

CREDITING

Crediting the past injustices in a person's life is an important form of acknowledgment. In attempting to be partial to each family member, the therapist may encounter situations in which it is difficult to side with a person's present behavior, for example, in the case of a parent who is being abusive or neglectful. In such cases it is useful to explore the past injustices which led to the parent being blind to the harm he or she is causing others. This process allows the therapist to be partial to the person without being partial to his or her present actions. The process of crediting provides the foundation for a trustworthy relationship with the therapist.

Debbie: Crediting Injustice (Vignette #2)

In this case, it was easy for the therapist to see Debbie's side and the difficulty of living with her mother's threats and the insecurity of being told that her forced departure was imminent. It was much more difficult to see her mother's side, because she was clearly failing to respond to her daughter's developmental needs. In fact, to appear to take her side, for example by blaming Debbie for being unappreciative of her mother, would not have been trustworthy behavior on the part of the therapist. It was difficult for the therapist to see a way to be partial to Ms. G for her present behavior. By taking a detailed family history, recorded in the form of a genogram, the therapist learned of the painful details of Ms. G's own childhood, discussed in the original presentation of this case. The therapist then was able to credit her for these past injustices, and so to be partial to her.

Ricky: Multidirected Partiality to a "Neglectful" Parent (Vignette #2)

In this case, as in that of Debbie, it was not difficult to be partial to the youngster who was in apparent need of medication in order to gain some satisfaction from his experience in the classroom and with peers. Again, as with Debbie, it was initially much more difficult to see the side of the father who prohibited the treatment his son apparently needed. In cases like this one, exploration of a parent's background can illuminate sources of injustice and provide the means for being partial to past injustice, if not to present behavior. Was this father denied medical treatment for his diabetes as a child? Was he perhaps punished in some way for being "sick"? Perhaps he, like his son, was told that he would just have to "live with" his condition.

LENDING WEIGHT

It can be useful for the therapist to lend his or her weight to the side of one person or another. In the case of marital therapy this may be the person who will be more capable of stating his or her side with the therapist's assistance. When working with families with young children the therapist may want to lend his or her weight in ways that make it easier for the child's side to be heard. I have used a number of techniques to accomplish this goal. These include using "yes" or "no" questions (e.g., "Is it hard for you to put what you are feeling into words?" "Does it seem unfair that school is so easy for your sister and so hard for you?" "Does it feel like you have to choose sides between your father and your mother?"); mind reading (e.g., "Are you worried that if you talk about your grandfather and how much you miss him that your mother will get upset and cry?"); and explicitly taking the child's perspective (e.g., "If I were Danny I think I might feel. . . ."). The therapist's lending his or her weight to a child does not mean that he or she has stopped being partial to the parents. From a contextual perspective, in fact, being partial to children is one way of helping parents. Situations involving abusive parents provide some of the most dramatic examples of this. A mother justified hitting her child, saying that the 9-year-old provoked her by verbal taunts and insults. The therapist reviewed with both the mother and the father that they had come to therapy to help their children. He also told the parents that he saw his work as trying to be helpful to all family members, but that when forced to choose between lending his weight to them or to their children, he would always choose the children, because by doing so he would be acting in the children's interest and also in the parents' interests as parents.

EXONERATION

This is not so much a technique applied by therapists as a process engaged in by clients with the help of the therapist. *Exoneration* refers to a process of working to understand one's parents and their developmental contexts well enough so that one may accept them with all their shortcomings. Exoneration is important because it allows people to be loyal to their parents on an overt level so that they are free to end a pattern of continued invisible loyalty. The foundation for helping adults to exonerate their parents is laid in the first session when therapists collect information regarding family history.

The process of exoneration is then facilitated by being partial to the parents of the adults with whom one is working, whether in individual, couples, or family sessions. Just as a therapist can strive to be partial to the divorced parent of a child, so can one strive to be partial to the distant or deceased parent of an adult. The following example is drawn from a case in which the original referral involved a parent's difficulties with young children.

Ms. H: Partiality to a Grandparent

Ms. H requested help in "managing" her children. In initial sessions, she acknowledged that she often overreacted to them in ways that tended to lead to escalating conflict. She also made it clear that she did not blame her children, and thought they were basically very well behaved, but that she found herself being too critical and harsh despite her best intentions. As the assessment phase continued and began to focus on individual and family history as well as on fairness issues, it became clear that her own childhood had been very difficult and marked by severe parentification. Ms. H blamed her mother for much of her childhood distress, and harbored a great deal of resentment toward her.

From the first session onward, the therapist expressed a great deal of interest in learning more about Ms. H's mother's background. This was expressed in subtle, as well as not so subtle, ways including statements such as, "I wonder what happened in your mother's growing up that led her to be so harsh and apparently so unaware of your needs growing up" and "I still think we need to learn more about your mother's early experience; do you think she would talk to you about this?" Even more explicit instances of partiality to Ms. H's mother included, "From what you have said about how your mother takes care of the grandchildren, she seems to be a very sweet person; do you think it possible that there is something we don't yet know about that made it hard for her to show this side to you when you were a child?"

Questions like these do not produce immediate or dramatic changes in the ways in which adults think about their parents. In my experience, though, repeatedly focusing on and showing interest in the side of adults' parents is often contagious, leading the adults to become more interested themselves. In the case just illustrated, Ms. H's patience with her children increased along with her understanding of her own mother's context. Such dramatic success is unusual, but it does occur frequently enough to make working toward exoneration a worthwhile goal.

HELPING PARENTS TO PROVIDE THEIR CHILDREN OPPORTUNITIES TO GIVE

The right to give is an important issue in contextual treatment. One of the important ways in which children give to their parents is through achievement in school. Bringing home papers with stars, and later quizzes, tests, and report cards with signs of accomplishment, is one way children have of giving something back to their parents, a reflection of the nurturance and support they have received. Children who excel in scholastic, athletic, and social arenas can give easily to their parents. Children like Tim, who have difficulties with scholastic accomplishment, may be deprived of this route to giving. Consider children whose difficulties may be mild (e.g., a mild reading disability or mild hyperactivity), moderate (e.g., having average intellectual potential in a family with many intellectually gifted children), or severe (e.g., having Down's syndrome, mental retardation, or cerebral palsy).

Some of these children may have natural strengths in other areas. For example, a child who has difficulty with reading may be a gifted athlete. If the child's athletic ability is appreciated in his or her family, then the child may find a way to give to his or her parents through accomplishment on the playing field. Some children, however, have difficulties in many areas. They may even have such serious difficulties that caring parents will give excessively to them, in an attempt to compensate for the injustice life has handed to them. And yet, these children have just as much need to give to others, particularly parents, as any other. In fact, perhaps they have a greater need and right to give in order to earn constructive entitlement and self-worth.

SUMMARY

Contextual therapy is an integrative, intergenerational, and resource-oriented approach to helping individuals, couples, and families. Contextual assessment and treatment proceed along four simultaneous dimensions: individual and family history, individual psychological issues, family transactions and power issues, and issues related to fairness in relationships. The approach integrates individual and family systems concepts and insights. It is historical in its emphasis on the importance of understanding how past harm which individuals have incurred can lead to a reliance on destructive entitlement and to a tendency to parentify others, especially their children. Another facet of the intergenerational aspect of the approach lies in the importance placed on helping adults to begin a process of exonerating their parents. The approach emphasizes the importance of helping people to identify and use resources for giving and receiving in themselves and their families. Contextual therapy tries to help people find a balance between what they give to others and what they receive from those others. Above all, the approach focuses on exploring resources in families, particularly intergenerational resources, for considerate giving and receiving.

REFERENCES

Ackerman, N. W. (1966). *Treating the Troubled Family*. New York: Basic Books.

Ackerman, N. W. (1967). Prejudice and scapegoating in the family. In G. H. Zuk & I. Boszormenyi-Nagy (Eds.), *Family Therapy and Disturbed Families*. Palo Alto: Science and Behavior Books.

Bateson, G., Jackson, D. D., Haley, J., & Weakland, J. H. (1956). Toward a theory of schizophrenia. *Behavioral Science, 1,* 251-254.

Boszormenyi-Nagy, I. (1965). A theory of relationships: Experience and transaction. In I. Boszormenyi-Nagy & J. L. Framo (Eds.), *Intensive Family Therapy* (pp. 33-86). New York: Brunner/Mazel.

Boszormenyi-Nagy, I. (1987). *Foundations of Contextual Therapy: Collected Papers of Ivan Boszormenyi-Nagy, M.D.* New York: Brunner/Mazel.

Boszormenyi-Nagy, I., Grunebaum, J., & Ulrich, D. (1991). Contextual therapy. In A. Gurman & D. P. Kniskern (Eds.), *Handbook of Family Therapy* (Vol. II, pp. 200-238). New York: Brunner/Mazel.

Boszormenyi-Nagy, I., & Krasner, B. (1986). *Between Give and Take: A Clinical Guide to Contextual Therapy*. New York: Brunner/Mazel.

Boszormenyi-Nagy, I., & Spark, G. M. (1973). *Invisible Loyalties*. New York: Harper & Row.

Bowen, M. (1966). The use of family therapy in clinical practice. *Comprehensive Psychiatry, 7,* 345-374.

Bowen, M. (1978). *Family Therapy in Clinical Practice.* New York: Jason Aronson.

Buber, M. (1957). Guilt and guilt feelings. *Psychiatry, 20,* 114-129.

Buber, M. (1958). *I and Thou* (2nd ed.) (R. G. Smith, Trans.). New York: Scribner's.

Cotroneo, M., & Krasner, B. R. (1976). Addiction, alienation, and parenting. *Nursing Clinics of North America, 2,* 517-525.

Erikson, E. H. (1963). *Childhood and Society.* New York: W. W. Norton.

Erikson, E. H. (1968). *Identity: Youth and Crisis.* New York: W. W. Norton.

Erikson, E. H. (1980). *Identity and the Life Cycle.* New York: W. W. Norton.

Fairbairn, W. R. D. (1954). *An Object Relations Theory of the Personality.* New York: Basic Books.

Flavell, J. H. (1977). *Cognitive Development.* New York: Prentice-Hall.

Framo, J. L. (1976). Family of origin as a resource for adults in marital and family therapy: You can and should go home again. *Family Process, 15,* 193-210.

Framo, J. L. (1982). *Explorations in Family and Marital Therapy.* New York: Springer.

Freud, A. (1946). *The Ego and the Mechanisms of Defense.* New York: International Universities Press.

Goldenthal, P. (1992, October). *Contextual Family Therapy for Disruptive Behavior Disorders.* Continuing Education Workshop presented at the annual meeting of the American Academy of Child and Adolescent Psychiatry, Washington, DC.

Guntrip, H. (1961). *Personality Structure and Human Interaction.* New York: International Universities Press.

Gurman, A. S., & Kniskern, D. P. (Eds.). (1981). *Handbook of Family Therapy.* New York: Brunner/Mazel.

Gurman, A. S., & Kniskern, D. P. (Eds.). (1991). *Handbook of Family Therapy* (Vol. II). New York: Brunner/Mazel.

Haley, J. (1976). *Problem Solving Therapy.* San Francisco: Jossey-Bass.

Hoffman, L. (1981). *Foundations of Family Therapy: A Conceptual Framework for Systems Change.* New York: Basic Books.

Jackson, D. D. (1957). The question of family homeostasis. *Psychiatric Quarterly, 31,* 79-90.

Levant, R. F. (1984). *Family Therapy: A Comprehensive Overview.* Englewood Cliffs, NJ: Prentice-Hall.

McGoldrick, M., & Gerson, R. (1985). *Genograms in Family Assessment.* New York: W. W. Norton.

Minuchin, S. (1974). *Families and Family Therapy.* Cambridge, MA: Harvard.

Piaget, J. (1963). *The Origins of Intelligence.* New York: W. W. Norton.

Piaget, J., & Inhelder, B. (1969). *The Psychology of the Child.* New York: Basic Books.

Rotter, J. B. (1954). *Social Learning and Clinical Psychology.* New York: Prentice-Hall.

Selvini-Palazzoli, M., Cecchin, G., Prata, G., & Boscolo, L. (1978). *Paradox and Counterparadox: A New Model in the Therapy of the Family in Schizophrenic Transaction.* New York: Jason Aronson.

Von Bertalanffy, L. (1968). *General Systems Theory: Foundation, Development, Applications.* New York: Braziller.

Watzlawick, P., Beavin, J. H., & Jackson, D. D. (1967). *Pragmatics of Human Communication: A Study of Interactional Patterns, Pathologies, and Paradoxes.* New York: W. W. Norton.

Watzlawick, P., Weakland, J., & Fisch, R. (1974). *Change: Principles of Problem Formation and Problem Resolution.* New York: W. W. Norton.

Wynne, L. C. (1965). Some indications and contraindications for exploratory family therapy. In I. Boszormenyi-Nagy & J. L. Framo (Eds.), *Intensive Family Therapy: Theoretical and Practical Aspects* (pp. 289-322). Hagerstown, MD: Harper & Row.

Wynne, L. C. (1988). *The State of the Art in Family Therapy Research: Comments and Recommendations.* New York: Family Process Press.

Wynne, L. C., Ryckoff, I. M., Day, J., & Hirsch, S. I. (1958). Pseudo-mutuality in the family relations of schizophrenics. *Psychiatry, 21,* 205-220.

Other Titles In Our
Practitioner's Resource Series

Each of these unique paperbound books focuses on a topic of critical and timely importance. These are concise, practice-oriented guidebooks designed to provide quick access to new concepts and applied clinical techniques.

Price Per Book: $9.95 Each.

Prices and availability subject to change without notice.

See Reverse Side For Ordering Information———▶

Order Form

Please Send Me The Following Books:

Quantity	Description of Product/Product Code	Price
SUBTOTAL		
FLORIDA ORDERS, ADD 7% SALES TAX		
SHIPPING		
TOTAL		

SHIPPING CHARGES
Up to $15.99 Order, Add $2.00 in US, $3.25 Foreign
$16 - $30.99 Order, Add $2.75 in US, $4.00 Foreign
$31 - $45.99 Order, Add $3.75 in US, $5.00 Foreign
$46 - $70.99 Order, Add $4.25 in US, $6.00 Foreign
Orders over $71, Add 7% in US, 10% Foreign
Call for charges for 1, 2, or 3 day US delivery or Foreign air

☐ Check or money order enclosed (payable to PRP; US funds only)

Charge my ☐ MasterCard ☐ Visa ☐ Discover ☐ American Express

Signature (Required if using credit card)_____

Card #_____ Expiration Date_____

Ship To:

Name_____
[Please Print]

Address_____

Address_____

City/State/Zip_____

Daytime Phone # (_____)_____

Order From:
Professional Resource Press • P.O. Box 15560 • Sarasota, FL 34277-1560
Telephone # 813-366-7913 • FAX # 813-366-7971

Would You Like Information On Our Other Publications?

For a copy of our latest catalog, please write, call, or fax the following information to the address and phone number listed below:

Name_____
[Please Print]

Address_____

Address_____

City/State/Zip_____

Telephone_____

Profession (check all that apply):

_____ Psychologist   _____ Mental Health Counselor
_____ Marriage and Family Therapist   _____ Psychiatrist
_____ School Psychologist   _____ Not in Mental Health Field
_____ Clinical Social Worker   _____ Other:_____

Professional Resource Press
P.O. Box 15560
Sarasota, FL 34277-1560

Telephone # 813-366-7913
FAX # 813-366-7971

1586